T0129128

Easley

EASLEY

★ ★ ★

Forrest N. Easley

iUniverse, Inc.
Bloomington

EASLEY

Copyright © 2013 Forrest N. Easley.

All rights reserved. No part of this book may be used or reproduced by any means, graphic, electronic, or mechanical, including photocopying, recording, taping or by any information storage retrieval system without the written permission of the publisher except in the case of brief quotations embodied in critical articles and reviews.

iUniverse books may be ordered through booksellers or by contacting:

iUniverse
1663 Liberty Drive
Bloomington, IN 47403
www.iuniverse.com
1-800-Authors (1-800-288-4677)

Because of the dynamic nature of the Internet, any web addresses or links contained in this book may have changed since publication and may no longer be valid. The views expressed in this work are solely those of the author and do not necessarily reflect the views of the publisher, and the publisher hereby disclaims any responsibility for them.

Any people depicted in stock imagery provided by Thinkstock are models, and such images are being used for illustrative purposes only.

Certain stock imagery © Thinkstock.

ISBN: 978-1-4759-9331-8 (sc)
ISBN: 978-1-4759-9330-1 (hc)
ISBN: 978-1-4759-9329-5 (e)

Library of Congress Control Number: 2013909959

Printed in the United States of America.

iUniverse rev. date: 5/29/2013

ACKNOWLEDGMENT

I wish to thank my wife, Marilyn, for her patience and understanding and for her advice and help with the test reading and comments and for assisting in the preparation of the manuscript. I, also, thank her for voluntarily spending all those hours alone to allow me the opportunity to prepare this autobiography.

I, also wish to thank the publisher for all their suggestions and extremely friendly partnership during the publishing phase of this work.

DEDICATIONS

I dedicate this work to all those who actually lived and died during those times and to each of their descendants and to all who are seriously interested in how life truly was during the time the old west was being settled.

I, also, wish to dedicate this work to those who participated in the War of all wars during recent times: WWII.

I also dedicate this work to all who are the veterans of WWII living and dead: the members of that "Greatest Generation" of which I am proud to a member. In addition, I wish to honor those who as we speak continue to give of themselves through work and prayer to protect our Freedoms and this beautiful land in which we all live and prosper and worship as we wish.

I remain faithful to my God and to America!

Coat of Arms

Easley

TABLE OF CONTENTS

⋆ ⋆ ⋆

Part Two

PROLOGUE

IN THE YEAR OF OUR LORD
ONE THOUSAND NINE HUNDRED NINETY EIGHT...

I begin recording for my children and grandchildren and their offspring (who, perhaps, may or may not have an interest in, or who may, at some point in time, develop an interest in) and for posterity, whom ever that might include, the historical events which, collectively, come together to form my own biographical story. These events occurred both before and during my own lifetime and are not intended to be entertaining, although many of them may cause various degrees of tittering for some readers. Neither are they intended to be embellishments of truths, but are included solely as truths as they happened in order to illustrate and to record the actual life experiences which collectively had great influence upon the development of me the person. This person was formed in a mold which taught me to have great inward feelings of tenderness, of honest love, of great sorrow for others' misfortune, of great and sacrificial self denial for the sake of my children, and an insatiable desire for learning ; all this built on a true and great and quiet and non-boisterous love for my God. Also, I have a quick willingness to suffer martyrdom that others might experience rewards and treasures ahead of myself because I had rather have my treasures "...stored up in Heaven."

Included are details of my parents' and grandparents' and experiences which evolved to form the family groups that migrated to the places they did, and which resulted in the people being born into the world in the places and under the conditions which were theirs. In addition to these details, are included the many stories resulting from their own pioneering experiences, their hardships, and their individual loyalties to this new country, America. This was evident by the very high quality and the intensity of their hard work, and their individualistic devotions that were extended to each of their individual trades and crafts and pursuits of life. This was particularly true for the folks on my mother's side of the family who had immigrated from Prussia around the year 1880. They had a far more ardent reason for leaving their homeland to look for freedom and new-found opportunities in this new "America." Perhaps this, also, is because these people were the actual generation which had left the motherland and had actually settled in, and then developed, the new areas of central Kansas, namely around Newton, Halstead, Moundridge, and Heston. In time, their interests spread to involve wheat farms and other interests alike over most of the state and beyond.

Unlike my mothers' side of the family tree, my father's forefathers had been in America for about eighteen generations or more. The Easley clan immigrated from Ireland and Scotland around the turn of the seventeenth century, and became quite ingrained in each area they traversed. Some became residents of the newly-formed New England colonies. Others chose to continue searching for their locations to settle, and still others continued migrating; some of those members of the Easley clan put down roots at each "rest" location during their westerly migration. Their people began settling in New England, mostly in what is now the Virginia and Pennsylvania areas, where some became educators, some became farmers, and some moved on. They migrated southward into North Carolina, where they settled for a while and started working in and utilizing the trades they had brought with them from the old country. These included textile workers and educators and inventors and farmers among others. One of their landmarks is the settlement of Easley, North Carolina, now a small city. But I want to digress a moment here to share a quotation from the ***Easley Genealogy***,

compiled and written by **J. D. Easley** , which is very interesting and of
great significance, and is quoted as follows:

Earliest history and the evolution of the name Easley.

*"What is known of the family prior to the flight to America so far as the
Easleys are concerned is tradition coupled with many historical facts.*

*It is believed that the family was first known in Southern Switzerland
where they were silk merchants. From Switzerland to France the move
was made sometime about the middle of the fifteenth century. After they
came to France, they were religiously Huguenots (persecuted French
Christians) and after the massacre of St. Bartholomew they fled to the
British Isles and the Netherlands. It seems the Easley contingent went
to England.*

*The name in Switzerland was spelled 'Islyn', and in France was
pronounced 'Else'. So the spelling was changed to 'Else' and was so
spelled in some of the early Virginia court records. For some reason not
known, a title with the prefix 'de' was awarded the family by some
French king for some service done or special act. It is told that there was
a coat of arms.* (NOTE: There is a coat of arms, and it is presented
on the Frontispiece of this autobiography.)

*So far as has been learned by close searching of Virginia court records,
Robert Easley was the first name and the only one of the name to the
Jamestown Colony. The best evidence that he was a Huguenot is that
he was granted land out of the allotment made to the French 'refugees'.
This grant was dated 20 October, 1704, and it was for 315 acres on
the east side of Reedy Creek on the James River in Henrico County,
Virginia.*

(Quoting further:)

Robert Else/Easley

*Robert was born in 1665 in England and married Ann Parker in either
England or in the new colony of Jamestown, Virginia in 1681. Ann's*

*grandmother was William Powell, Lt. Governor of Jamestown in 1611.
Below is a short history in the Jamestown Colony:*

*Jamestown Virginia. The first permanent English settlement in North
America was Jamestown, Virginia, established in 1607. The colony was
the project of the London Company, which was chartered in the previous
year by King James I. Under the leadership of John Smith of the London
Company, the colony barely survived famine, Native American attacks,
and an outbreak of malaria. New settlers and supplies arrived in 1610,
and commercial development of tobacco crops finally enabled the colony
to thrive. The marriage in 1614 of colonist John Rolfe and Pocahontas,
the daughter of an Algonquian chief, brought several years of peace with
the Native Americans. (Jamestown." Microsoft Encarta Encyclopedia
99, copyright 1993-1998 Microsoft Corporation. All rights reserved.)*

The children of Robert Easley and Ann Parker were:

1. John, married Mary Benskin 1711.
2. Warham.
3. Margaret.
4. Elizabeth.
5. William, born 1692, married _____ Pyrant.
6. Robert."

The end of quotation.

But some of the Easley clan felt they needed go farther west to
discover different things and experience the adventure of starting in a
brand new place. They eventually moved into Kentucky and Tennessee.
Of course, the younger males married into other clans at each place and
the great intermix was on. My father's father, James Easley, married
Katherine May from Tennessee and moved further to the west and
wound up in eastern Texas.

These were a nomad-type farming people who did not own their
own farms but rented farms from others on the "shares," giving the
owner one fourth of the crop in payment for the use of the farm for their
own purposes. This was an ideal way for those people to move about

from year to year without the burden of actually owning land, and it gave them the freedom to earn a living and yet look for their dream destination where they would eventually put down roots and become land owners and members of the new-found community, wherever that was to be.

The admixture of the two totally different cultures, Dad's and Mom's, had a very important influence on my upbringing, and the communities and social environments that we lived in during my young life stamped me forever and made me a person so unique unto myself. However, only through hard work and devoted efforts, and by the drench of sweat from my own brow over many years, did I managed to escape into a more culturally satisfying lifestyle which allowed me to develop a life with more personal meaning than had I not tried to make that move . This seems to be the thread that weaves its way throughout my life span that seems to be parallel to, if not basic to, most of my ambitions and goals except for one.

It has always been basic to my life's purpose to live such that I would be guaranteed a place at God's right hand after completing my earthly preparation for God's Heavenly place by living each hour here according to His instructions instead of by mans' biased religious teachings, to the best of my ability, and then some. So this was the beginning of my looking for the real *truth* of God's instructions and not by depending totally upon the hypocritical teachings of some so called churches. First hand, as a child and young man, I witnessed the constant selfishness and the know-it-all attitudes of ministers and the misinterpretation of "God's Word", so I began my own search. After all, I understood that this is a matter between only God and myself. And as far as *truth* goes, most churches and preachers fully believe that their interpretation is the only truth, but Jesus told us that HE is the truth. This, for some reason they can't understand. I do, however, and I shall receive Jesus' blessing for believing in Him and only in His definition, not man's.

This, in fact, IS the thread basic to all my consciousness and is surrounded by the other basic thread afore mentioned. So, then, I started many years ago as a young man mentally planning to record my life's story. I did not care to record it for monetary benefit, nor for purposes of vanity nor to "save others", but, as said in the beginning, for purposes of passing on to my descendants and others the actual high points as well as low points of interest and the actual key biographical factors which caused me to be Forrest Newitt Easley.

PART ONE

The Nineteenth Century Was Drawing to a Close,
And With it Came Hope Because of an Opportunity
For the Poor Farmer to Homestead His own Place
To be His Own "King."

Although it was the Ending of the
Nineteenth Century, it was...

CHAPTER I

* * *

"... A BEGINNING!"

I grew up on a dry farm in the very center of the then brand-new state of New Mexico which is situated in the southwestern and very scenic portion of the United States. My father's parents, James and Katherine Easley had migrated there from East Texas where they share cropped and raised eleven children on a farm where they raised peanuts and cotton and sorghum cane near Mount Pleasant. In this hot, humid country, the work was hard and backbreaking, and the suffering in those days from the millions of mosquitos and flies and the associated illnesses for the meager existence the land provided seemed so unfair and unrewarding. Also, their family had increased in size and the health and well-being of the younger members of the family was of great concern. So after several years of hard work, sweat, and struggling to provide for the large family, Grandpa Jim began searching for a better way to survive, now that the years were taking their toll on him. Then, somehow, he heard that the federal government was setting aside land in the new state of New Mexico which could be filed on and claimed by citizens of the United States under the Homestead Act.

The main requirement was that the claim owners had to spend a minimum of 250 dollars (at that time) on improvements and they had to live on the property three out of the five years it took to earn a patent to the land from the Bureau of Land Management. So the James Easley family loaded up their belongings into railroad boxcars they had leased and headed west. They put their personal things into one end of a boxcar, lived in the other end of that car, and put their animals and farm machinery into another boxcar. At last, in the newly formed state of New Mexico, he would be permitted to homestead on 640 acres of government land which would become his own after only five years to "prove up." And, they would have all their possessions with them and not have to replace them.

They were, however, unable to travel the entire distance by rail, so they had their leased boxcars placed on a siding in the West Texas town of Childress. Here they could unload from the train cars their wagons and teams, their cows, furniture and personal items they were bringing west with them. They could work for a while to earn more money to finance the rest of their move to central New Mexico. However, misfortune was to overtake Grandpa and cause a serious setback in their plans. It was a terrible accident that befell Grandpa Jim, and had he not been a very strong minded individual with a determination of steel, he would have had his life's dream of owning his own farm smashed to bits right then and there! But not Grandpa! Here's what happened on that bright sunny day which was so filled with his plans for moving into their new temporary home in Childress

As the family was off-loading their possessions from the train cars, their wagon shipped from its moorings as they were taking it out of the boxcar. It rolled over Grandpa breaking his back between his shoulders. Of course, this was quite a serious situation because little or no medical and surgical help existed within their grasp, and all treatment and healing was at the hands of Grandma Katherine and the children. Grandpa lay helpless in his bed in the boxcar until he could heal enough to be moved into a house somewhere. But Grandpa Jim was handicapped only physically. His mind was as sharp and quick as always and with a groan and a smile, he, from his sickbed, managed to locate a farm which could be rented on the "shares."

They had never been to New Mexico, let alone to the land they hoped to homestead. So Grandpa Jim, as the grandchildren later called him, rented the farm there in Childress and put the children in school there. The children and Grandma did the actual work of farming and Grandpa Jim supervised from his sickbed until such time that he could manage to sit up with the help of improvised splints and braces they had designed for him. Their combined success was admirable and, they managed to save enough money from their farming efforts during the next couple of years to make the next long leg of the move to his "promised land." But since there were no farms to rent or work to be had in this particular part of New Mexico yet, he decided to go, instead, to the Ruidoso and Alto areas in the White Mountains northwest of the town of Roswell on the upper Hondo River.

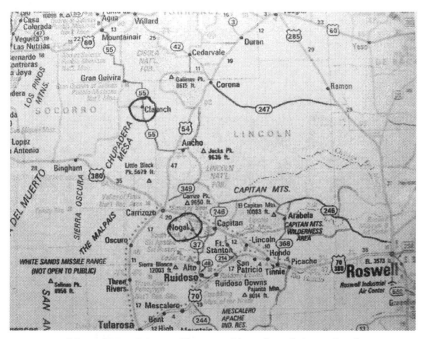

*Map of New Mexico Showing Claunch and Areas South
Including the Ruidosa Area Where Grandpa First Located
Temporarily Prior to Homesteading Near Claunch.*

By this time, his back had become severely bent forward and his shoulders very severely stooped which shortened his stature of a tall man of over six feet to a man of some six or seven inches shorter. But with the help of his entire family that accompanied him west, his dreams were as vivid and intense as ever, and he continued healing and working doggedly to fulfill them.

This area was situated in the high mountains just below the east face of a 12,000-foot snow-capped mountain called Mount Baldy. Several creeks headed in the nearby canyons leading downward from the mountain peak (also known in Spanish as Sierra Blanca). This was a very beautiful area which comprised numerous small valleys conducive to various types of farming. There, large apple orchards and construction projects were in operation and one could find employment, at least for the short term. This was especially true around the village of Alto, to the northwest of Ruidoso, where the Southern Pacific Railroad had built a dam across Eagle Creek to provide soft water for the locomotives which pulled the trains on the SP Railroad from El Paso, Texas north through Carrizozo about 30 miles to the west and on north to far distant points. This was, and is, a semi-arid area and soft water had to be piped to the railroad down from the mountains through huge wooden pipes which were wrapped with steel wire. So, in reality, the area was growing and people were moving there from points unknown to begin new lives just as Grandpa Jim's family was doing.

Things were in his favor, however. He had learned that a postmaster was needed at the brand new Nogal (pronounced: no-gal) Post Office a few miles to the north. He applied. He was hired and wasted no time in establishing himself in the new position of Postmaster. Grandpa Jim, being the outgoing and friendly person that he was, soon became well acquainted with all the residents in the area, and was intrigued by a suggestion that was made by his family and friends. Letting no grass grow under his feet, so to speak, he thought the suggestion was a very good one, so he opened a general store in connection with the post office. He soon learned that the family members, who were still at home, could take care of the business at the store and post office, thus giving him free time to pursue his dream of become a homesteader. Grandpa Jim was more sentimental, I think, than was Grandma. Oh, Grandma loved her flower garden and wild flowers of the mountain valleys, but Grandpa watched things like rainbows and the birds flying south and again, in the spring, back north again. Grandpa loved to look from his favorite high mountain vista near beautiful Alto and view the early morning rainstorms taking place far to the west of him in the huge valley below, in the valley of the *malpais* volcanic lava flow which covered many square miles in area. Invariably, these early morning rain storms would be bathed in the bright sunrise that created the most beautiful rainbows that seemed to last forever until the sun passed from its refractive position in the heavens.

As Grandpa contemplated the area where he should homestead he thought, "Perhaps God is trying to tell me something here." He, of course knew all about that so-called pot of gold at the end of the rainbow, but he wasn't looking for a pot of gold, he was looking for them a new home. "Could this be it?" he said to himself.

Grandpa Jim by this time had become so inspired that he planned to travel by wagon to the homestead land site of interest about 45 miles northwest of Carrizozo just to the east of the Chupadera (pronounced: choo-pah-day-rah) Mesa as soon as he possibly could make the arrangements. The government had already approved the Homestead Act and had released vacant land in the entire area, as well as most all of the vacant, non-school-section land of the western United States. This was bringing in homesteaders from all over the country. The only requirement was that they were citizens and that they prove up on the land. The U.S. Patent Office would then issue a patent to the land to the homesteader. The land parcels were 640 acres in size, or any fraction thereof by quarter sections. That is, one could file on either 160 acres, 320 acres, 480 acres *or* a full section, 640 acres. It is also important to note here that there were some locations, especially in the mid-western part of the country where only 160 acres was the maximum allowed to be filed upon. Some present-day people, who weren't around back then, are of the mindset that homesteading was open only to veterans of wars. However, this was not true entirely, except that veterans had a priority in the pecking order of filers. Grandpa Jim was not a war veteran and had no problem with the filing application.

Grandpa Jim had chosen the land of his choice quickly and filed claim on it. Plans were made with the U.S. Land Office in Las Cruces to begin proving up on the place. This all took considerable time, but he persisted and within a year or so began constructing the house and barn and fences on the place. All went very well. Soon enough money was saved from the postmaster's salary and profits from the store so they began to make plans to sell the business and move to the new homestead, the final leg of their long journey to their new dream place of their very own.

But, to back up for a moment, while the family was still at Childress, Dad had decided he was finished with school by the time he finished the ninth grade, so he joined the U.S. Army. Dad's sister, Maude, had decided to marry and move to Fort Worth, Texas where she spent the remainder of her life, passing away in 1936 with sugar diabetes. Dad's sister, Lena, married Scott Hagee, son of a pioneer covered-wagon immigrant family, and together she and Uncle Scott built and operated the *Hollywood Café* in Ruidoso after the folks had moved to that area. Another brother of Dad's, Jess, stayed with Grandpa Jim and made the move to the homestead with his parents. Uncle Jess had married a schoolmate, Ethyl Gaines, whom he had known from the days when they lived in East Texas. But when Grandpa Jim moved into his newly homesteaded place in New Mexico, Uncle Jess and his new bride decided to homestead a place of their own next to Grandpa's joining him on the west side. This worked out very nicely because he not only could help Grandpa with work around the place, but it provided neighbors and close proximity of family members. Uncle Jess and Aunt Ethyl raised a family of four on this homestead. There was the eldest son, Glen, the eldest daughter, Doris, another daughter, Dorothy, and a younger daughter, Bobby Lee. Later on, there was another son, Jess, Jr.

Dad's youngest sister, Jewel, was only about fourteen at the time Grandpa Jim made the big move to the new homestead and was the pride and joy of my grandparents. She was a very pretty girl and very well behaved. Above all, she loved God with all her being, and never missed her daily talks with her Lord. Aunt Jewel grew up to be a beautiful young woman and, later, a wonderful wife to Mack Wells whom she had met while living in the White Mountains at Alto. I believe he was originally from the small town of La Luz and whose parents were neighbors to the Bonnie family, the parents of William Bonnie ("Billy-the-Kid"). After their marriage, they homesteaded on another section of their own about two miles northwest of Grandpa's. Their section was located about three miles southeast of Gran Quivera where in later years Uncle Mack owned the old "Miller Store" and Post Office.

There, Aunt Jewel bore him two sons, Mack Jr. and Vess Wells before passing away leaving Uncle Mack to raise the boys. She was as near a perfect Christian woman and lady as I have ever known anyplace. I am certain the Lord was so pleased with her that He decided to take her to be with Him at the early age of twenty six. The boys grew up to be well adjusted and honorable men, Mack Jr. to be a line supervisor for the El Paso petroleum pipe line, which was later built through the area passing just north of their farm, and Vess a respected and responsible member of the U.S. armed forces in Germany. Aunt Jewel was buried in the White Lake cemetery which joined their farm on the southwest corner. She was to be joined many years later by her husband, Uncle Mack who was buried at her side and a headstone marks their final resting place forever.

Grandpa Jim spent considerable time on the place readying it for the family and laying out the field and fences. He also prepared a temporary dwelling to protect him from the elements while he was building the house to move his family into later on. The temporary shelter was merely a small room dug into the ground which he covered with cedar logs and lumber and dirt. These dugouts were quite common among the homesteaders because they were fast to construct and provided very good shelter while the more permanent house was being built. Later, the dugout would become the cellar where they would store their canned goods and potatoes and turnips and whatever else they chose to store in there. As the days passed, things took shape and the house became reality, and the long trip was made to get his family and to wind up his affairs in that community. This included finding a replacement postmaster. Finally, all his business affairs were finalized and the move to their new home on the homestead was made. The family settled in and each family member pitched in and soon the place became livable and ready to begin getting the preparations for farming underway.

Barbed wire fences were built to keep stray sheep and cattle out and to keep their animals in. Also, they plowed up many acres of their land into a field on which the family planted crops of pinto beans and corn and millet. They also had brought their hogs along from East Texas as well as their cows and horses. They had a cow or two for milk and some to sell and the offspring to butcher for domestic meat. Grandma loved to raise her chickens and tend the flocks of them she had. She would have nothing else but white leghorn chickens because she claimed they laid many more eggs than any other kind of chicken. Grandpa, on the other hand, didn't like white leghorns because he claimed the chicken hawks could spot them easier because of their white color. However, it's needless to say here who won that debate.

But, ever since he had settled there back in the mid '20s, Grandpa Jim Easley was considered a good farmer and usually produced as much or more than the run of the mill neighbors did, who were often after him for his *secrets*. Of course, the only so called secrets he used were a lot of work and sweat and numerous kids to work in the field. He also relied religiously on the *Farmer's Almanac*. At first, going was rough and crops did not produce as much as later on because it usually took a couple of years for the soil to get used to being tilled in order to keep the weeds down and "hold" the moisture from the spring and summer rains. As newcomers were destined to learn, dry farming was much different and more pleasurable than irrigated farming, but it takes a bit more skill and knowledge to conserve moisture and yet let the soil "breathe". Grandpa Jim already was a master at this farming discipline and had no trouble with the idea of dry farming. So shortly, Grandpa Jim was so thrilled with their new farm and new home that he began writing letters to Dad to encourage him to sell his newly built home in Newton, Kansas and move to a homestead near him. It is of great interest to note at this time that in order for Grandpa Jim to mail his letters, he had to make the 14-mile trip by wagon and team over prairie and through cedar-timbered hills without any established roads, except for cow trails, to the Post Office in the very small village of Gran Quivera. This was the only so-called post office in the entire area for a distance of some 40 miles. Gran Quivera was a small village that sprung up in this particular place because of its proximity to the ruins of the centuries-old Indian mission and regional Indian trading center which was now uninhabited except for "Doc" Smith who was a self-proclaimed curator and made himself feel very important by "digging" there and showing the place to an occasional passerby.

The Gran Quivera Indian Ruins in 1926. The car is a 1926 Nash
That Grandpa Malleis Owned and Had Driven From Newton
Down to Our Homestead For a Visit. We Went On an Outing to
Visit the Ruins and Have a Picnic. Grandpa is Behind the Car.

In the picture, Grandpa Malleis is seen standing behind the car, but if one looks carefully, they can see my little legs on the other side of the car as well. I "...was two years old and hiding from the person taking the picture," they said later.

Years later, the National Park Service saw fit to add it to their list of National Monuments. Also, shallow water existed in this geologic basin which provided good water to anyone who could drill a well a hundred feet deep. Water elsewhere around was from 300 to 1000 feet deep and required a sizable windmill or gasoline-engine pump jack to raise the water to the surface. So land in this small basin around Gran Quivera was a treasure, indeed, and was, obviously, the reason the Indians settled here, too, some 400 years ago. Never-the-less, the trip to mail letters was a long and arduous one which required most of the day to accomplish.

Of course, Dad had no talents in the farming arena and could have lived his entire life without learning any. But Grandpa Jim was persistent. Dad and Mom were certainly confused and unsure about selling what they together had planned and built in Newton. But, on the other hand, they didn't want to pass up a golden opportunity to homestead on 640 acres of beautiful land in the new state of New Mexico. If, in fact, they should like the situation in New Mexico, then they felt it would be a huge mistake to pass it up. They felt it most likely would be wise to give up the good job Dad had as Second Chair barber in a well-established barber shop which had a continuing and permanent clientele. The owner operated the "first" chair. But after much talking and debating and evaluation, they finally decided to make a preliminary trip to look the situation over. Also, they decided to "kill two birds with one stone" and make a vacation of the trip and go by way of East Texas and visit friends and relatives and rekindle memories from Dad's childhood. They decided, also, to follow the route the Easley family took when they migrated west in order to visit old friends and relatives all the way to New Mexico. So plans were made.

Our New 1923 Ford Milady's Coupe That Took Us to East Texas and New Mexico. Mom can be Seen Holding Me in the Driver's Seat.

CHAPTER 2
* * *
MEMORIES REVISITED

As Dad readied the 1923 Model "T" Ford "Milady's" coupe, Mom busied herself trying to get me bathed and dressed plus a hundred other chores a mother does getting ready to leave for a trip. Of course, Dad's chores weren't to be snickered at either. But changing the oil and greasing and oiling the oil cups, checking the differential gear case oil, tire pressure, tightening lug bolts, adjusting wheel bearings, and washing the car weren't nearly as frustrating as all the "little" jobs Mom was left to do. Packing space available in that little Ford coupe was at a premium, but nevertheless, a certain amount of "stuff" was absolutely necessary for a trip of the magnitude they had planned. Baby things for me, food for us all, extra gasoline and oil for the car, extra tires, bedding, a shelter for camping out, parts for the car, clothing, plus all the numerous little things so necessary, required a given amount of space even for the very most efficient packer. But Henry Ford was a very intelligent man and had insights one must admire and envy. These included making running boards large enough and providing optional luggage carriers for them to haul most of the items on the running boards that were required for traveling long distances, not to mention tools.

But soon everything was readied and the family headed out. Now since the Easley clan started out from Eastern Texas, Dad thought they would strike out for Mount Pleasant.

"We'll drive down toward east Texas where I was born and spent my youngest years. We can look up relatives there and see places and things of importance to my childhood," Dad explained to Mom.

On the route chosen, we traveled south from Newton, to Wichita, into Oklahoma, and on into north Texas. Mom told me later on when I was much older, the reality of that part of the trip. "The only main roads across these states were graded dirt roads except for inside the towns," she explained.

"The roads there were usually made of paving brick, but ended at the city limits," Dad said. But, I myself remember very little of this trip. However, I DO remember two events, one quite clearly and the other just vaguely. I will share them here as I remember them:

The first event I personally remember about this trip is what occurred when we crossed the Red River between Oklahoma and Texas just south of Hugo, Oklahoma. Dad drove up to this big river, or, at least it looked *big* to me. Later I was told it was the Red River. He stopped the car on the road and was waiting for cars to proceed toward us across the river. There was no bridge, just a shallow place where cars could cross one at a time using a specific narrow path through the water. "We'll just wait here for a while to see if we can get across."

I remember Mom and Dad talking and saying there was "quick sand" out there. He pointed to the top of a car's windshield which was sticking up above the moving water. "That car missed the solid road," Dad told us.

The road, he said, had been packed down by the traffic and the car had gone off the road by mistake and sank into the quick sand. It had all but disappeared into the river bottom except for the last few inches of the windshield. I remember Dad started driving into the water and I became very frightened of the water. I remember crying and saw the water alongside the car really close to me and I thought I was going to fall into it. I remember us passing the sunken car just to my side of our car as we passed. I remember us driving up and out of the water and we stopped to look back at the sunken car. Mom explained, "I think the folks standing on the bank of the river are the ones who were in the car and had gotten out and waded out of the river."

During the following years, my folks would tell of the trip when visiting other people and tell about the car in Red River, and, on occasion, I remember me saying, "I saw it too."

Dad recalled that the road from the Red River to Mount Pleasant seemed very long and travel seemed slow, but even more so since he was returning after so many, many years away. As he drove along the graded dirt roads he carefully caught himself watching out for the chug holes and deep ruts that might grab the front wheels and cause him to lose control of the car. Being a very good driver with several years' experience made the task much easier than it would have been for a neophyte. Even with such poor roads, we did travel that entire distance without even a flat tire, Dad said. The '23 Ford was performing so well, and Dad was so proud of his new car.

Many relatives lived in the surrounding counties of Titus, Franklin, Camp, Hopkins, Cass, Delta, and in Cooke County to the west. These are the counties where a couple of Dad's siblings, his uncles and aunts and grandparents lived. Most of them were share croppers, but some owned their own businesses. So Dad and Mom made the big swing of the counties visiting these folks and becoming reacquainted after all those years apart. The First World War seemed to have divided families for one reason or another, as does every large war. Although I remember none of this visiting of relatives, I was told the stories many times down through the ensuing years and they seem so real to me even now. One of the stories, I do remember is the "second" story I iterated above. This is a memory of an evening after a day's drive,

Dad pulled over into a small grassy park alongside a small river and near the road. There were tall pecan trees to provide shade and protection from rain in the event that should occur during the night. The folks planned to stop there for the night and roll out their bed roll. The part I particularly remember is Dad preparing supper by the light of the car's less-than-brilliant headlights and a coal oil lantern.

Dad got out the gasoline camp stove and pumped up the air pressure in its fuel tank, and let fuel run into the primer cup which he lit to preheat the generator. *(I don't remember this bit of detail, but that's what one had to do in order to light the stove, which, by the way, I still possess.)* Dad put the skillet on the stove and got the lard and the sack of farm fresh eggs he had just bought down the road at a roadside store. As he and Mom visited and discussed the day's events and things that remained to be done that night before retiring, Dad began cracking and breaking the eggs into the skillet for supper. This done, he very efficiently busied himself with small items such as helping Mom get the plates ready, the silverware and so forth.

Abruptly, Mom asked, "What's that awful smell?" "I don't know, Elda." Dad replied. (Dad had never called Mom by any endearing name that I can remember.) He looked around for a dead animal on the ground. He figured that maybe he had parked the car over a dead animal of some kind. No luck! No dead animal. He looked and looked. Finally, he followed his nose and ended up above the skillet. "Elda, look at this!" he said. "Look at what's in the skillet. It's dead chickens. Those eggs were hatching!"

The weather was unusually hot and, of course, country stores at that time had no method of refrigeration because of their low income and the high prices of the newly developed electric refrigeration equipment. The eggs had been very warm, and there was no way of telling just how long they had been in the store subsequent to being laid. Yes, the eggs had begun forming little chicks and were well on the way toward incubation.

Mom walked over and looked into the skillet as Dad held the lantern near it. Mom started to get sick and Dad grabbed the skillet and threw the contents into the river. Needless to say, we went to bed without our suppers that night. I remember I went to bed crying because I was very hungry. The last thing I remember that day is Mom holding me to her breast patting me and crying as I cried myself to sleep. I loved Mom so very much, she was always my best friend, even to her death in 1989 at age 87. "I miss you, Mom."

The trip west served its purpose and the folks were anxious to make the move to New Mexico, but Mom did have her reservations.

In early1926, Dad sold the home in Newton and shipped our things by train to the Santa Fe Railway depot in the small farming town of Mountainair, New Mexico about 40 miles to the northwest of our new homestead. Dad and Mom loaded me, at age eighteen months, into our 1923 Ford coupe along with enough things to make the 600-mile trip to our new homestead. That trip turned into a story of its own and will be told later, but making the actual break from Newton was an extremely difficult decision for the folks to make.

Dad, had barbered there in Newton, a railroad town of some importance, during the years following the First World War, and stood in good stead with his railroad customers who held him high as a fine barber. In those days, a good barber was considered a "fine" barber by the professionalism and mastery of his trade, the smooth shaves, the hot towels, the sharp razors, the neatness of a haircut, and the amount of accrued local and political news he had to exchange during the customer's visit to the barber shop. It was extremely difficult for him to break away from these friends and business partners and those established customers and make such a drastic move into the unknown way of life where he had absolutely no expertise...farming a homestead out west! But the steady barrage of letters from the folks in New Mexico got to be too much for Dad's resistance to the idea of moving to be near his father on our own homestead. He gave in and started making plans, being the head of the family, for the big move.

This, however, all came about with much sorrow for Mom, who had been born Elda Marie Malleis in the small town of Moundridge, Kansas. Her parents moved soon after to the nearby town of Newton where she was raised and received her schooling. She had absolutely no idea as a young girl, or even when she married Dad, that she would ever in her lifetime have to give up the High-German upbringing and lifestyle to wind up having to live on a pioneer homestead in New Mexico.

The Malleis clan had settled around the central Kansas area during the 1880s as a result of their decade-long plan to leave Germany and immigrate to America. This plan resulted from their fear of their being ostracized by the then Emperor of Prussia (Germany), Kaiser Wilhelm. It had taken them several years to prepare for and to migrate from the northern part of Prussia, near the town of Elbing, to the southwest part of Germany where they took up temporary residence in France until they could all assemble there and then make further plans to cross France to obtain passage on ships to New York.

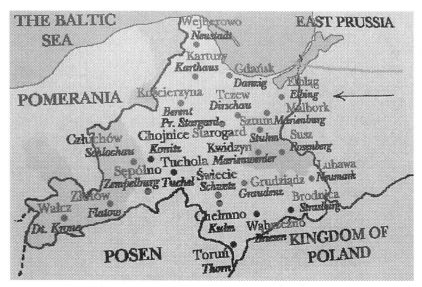

*Map of Old Prussia (Pronounced by Grandpa Malleis as "Proosshia)
From Whence the Malleis Clan Immigrated Along With Hundreds of Others.*

They brought with them all their personal treasures and memorabilia of their friends and homes left behind. Part of the clan were of the High-German culture and some were of the Low-German culture, resulting in some variances in customs and language. These variances were to continue indefinitely. Even at this writing, the name is pronounced differently, although spelled the same. For example the Low-German clan settled to the west of Newton and to the south of Kansas City, Missouri and on homesteads in Oklahoma, and pronounced their name as (mah-lees). The High-German group around Newton pronounce their name (ma-lie-es). Among all these people were not only relatives but many, many friends and neighbors. The people were of all trades. Most of them were rather clannish because of the harsh country they had wound up in, and because of their language barrier in this new land. However, some of them, relatives as well, decided to make the break and move either farther on or spread out into different areas which isolated themselves inadvertently from the rest of the families and friends. But the trip west from the east coast, the place of their debarkation, was one of much interest and filled with experiences which brought them up short and introduced them to the realities of the "new world!"

Most all of the farmers, led by the wealthy Workentein family, who brought with him the hard red winter wheat from Prussia and planted it in the area to introduce it for the first time in America. This wheat has, over the years, become the famous *hard* winter wheat used today to make the finest flour, and is known as *winter wheat.*

So Mom had grown up among these people and was truly one of them, one of the High-German social members. She loved them all and was related to a lot of them in both classes and had no prejudice either way. As a result, she was very respected by everyone and loved dearly by as many. So any idea of ever leaving this part of Kansas was a major decision, indeed! But she had met Dad during the very early twenties who had just graduated from Barber College in Ogden, Utah and had made the move to Newton. Dad put it this way: "My cousin happened to live in Ogden, Utah, where I attended barber school, and told of a very good friend who lived in Newton that owned a very nice barber shop near the Santa Fe Railroad Station and shops and had a very good clientele. He recommended I look him up for employment. So I did just that," Dad said.

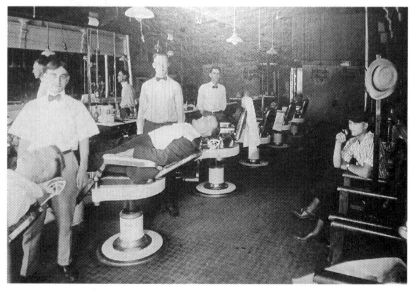

Bert Schifflet's Barber Shoppe in Newton Where Dad
(Second Chair) Was Well Established (1922-1926)

I'm not certain how he met Mom, but they did meet and were married in 1923. I was born to them on March 20, 1924 at the Harvey County Hospital. "We had built a new home there and were very nicely settled it seemed, Mom said."

Oscar and Elda (Malleis) Easley Wedding Picture, 1923.

So having to up and leave this new home and also to have to leave all these people and all her childhood friends and all her church family and, most importantly, her German-born father (her mother, Katherine, had passed away in 1923), made the move a matter of great sorrow which she never got over.

Baby Forrest Newitt Easley at age Three Months in His Favorite Buggy.

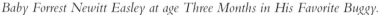

However, a few years after our migration west, things were to get a bit more palatable for Mom and she managed to adapt somewhat to the pioneer lifestyle on our new home place. But at that time in her life, she was leaving her lifelong home, and was off to build a brand new life and home with her new family in a far off place she had but only heard about. And behold! This was a brand new state, also! It was full of adventure and possibilities. However, most of the women in those days seemed very loyal to their husbands' leadership and adapted themselves wholeheartedly, a trait which in later generations has all but disappeared! This excellent quality proved to be extremely important in the years following to maintain family unity and help perpetuate Dad's drive, especially during difficult times. But the moving trip was at hand.

"The '23 Ford Coupe ran fine the entire trip, which lasted several long and tiresome days," Dad said later.

Dad and Mom and I had left Newton during early spring, 1926, very early in the morning darkness using the car's headlights to light their way. The gravel road they traveled led out of Newton west to Hutchinson then southwest to Pratt. At that point, Dad joined what is now highway 54 and headed west toward Liberal which was located in the extreme southwestern part of Kansas and was a very long stretch of road which had very little in the way of conveniences. In those days most all the roads had not yet been paved and some of those dirt roads were smoother than others. Not all of the creeks and rivers had bridges or improved crossings of any kind. Ferry crossings were common on the larger streams, but the more shallow rivers and streams had to be crossed by the seat of one's pants, so to speak. If there was a farm nearby one could negotiate to have the farmer and his team pull the car across if the car could not make it on its own. Dad was a very good driver, however, and the '23 Ford was almost new and in excellent condition for the trip. Mom recalled that after we had been traveling a day or so, the Ford's engine began to miss.

It needs to be explain here that Mom was a fairly decent mechanic herself, and had a keen ear for mechanical anomalies.

Of course, this was normal for Fords because they had four ignition coils underneath the dash, one for each cylinder, each of which was equipped with vibrator ignition points which would burn or pit under continuous driving. This meant that Dad would have to stop the car and remove the points from the guilty coil and file the points to a new shiny surface again. Onward and forward! In a few hours...do it again! Then in the next town, purchase a new set of points and we were ready for another day or two driving. However, it didn't take Dad long to learn that if an extra coil or two were stowed under the seat at the space at the end of the gas tank, it could quickly be brought out to replace the ailing coil while on the move without even stopping. So it was the usual thing to observe several spare coils in most all model T Fords during those times.

When night came and Dad tired of driving, the folks began looking for a town on the map to secure lodging for the night if there was a tourist court, or at a private home by asking around until they found a willing home owner. But it also needs to be said here that the folks had brought with them the necessary bedding and clothing and food and other necessary items to spend the night along the road. So in the event lodging could not be obtained, they would select a desirable spot along the road and simply pull over for the night. The gasoline, two burner camp stove was also brought along to cook on. Of course, I personally don't remember much of that trip, but I do remember one thing quite clearly. That was when we were driving along when all at once a "very large" locomotive overtook and passed us by as though we were just standing still. I remember it well because the engineer blew his whistle at us as he was even with our car, and both the fireman and engineer leaned out the window and waved at us. Mom told me later that I screamed "bloody murder", as she put it, when the train whistle blew because it was extremely loud since the tracks were so close to the road. I have been told this story by my folks many times, and I enjoyed their relating it to me every time as though it were the first time. My parents are both gone now, but their stories of my youth are still so very vivid and sometimes bring a tear to my eye.

As the little Ford purred along the more-or-less "smooth" road westward, we passed many places of interest that either caused Dad to pull over to visit, or call Mom's attention to as we drove. One such place was the actual World's Largest Hand Dug Well located at Greensburg, Kansas. This is supposed to be the very largest hand dug well in existence, even to date. Dad was always interested in such things and wanted, always, to share them with everyone else, even when they may not be that interested. But Mom was a person of great curiosity and enjoyed those things also. However, the fact was that Mom had already visited the World's Largest Well before. Turns out that Mom's parents had on many, many occasions traveled Kansas quite thoroughly during Mom's growing up and had, in fact, visited most every place of any interest at all within the states of both Kansas and Colorado.

But that made an excellent camping spot for the night, so they unpacked things necessary and made camp. The well, incidentally, was well known for its fine water. The small town nearby provided the necessary items we needed such as fresh bread and non-perishables to be taken on the road the next day.

Along the way as we proceeded westward, farmers were seen working their fields with huge steam tractors pulling many plows behind them. Dad was intrigued by these sights and talked at length about the day he would be able to do the same things on our new homestead in New Mexico. Again, I remember nothing of these sights, only Dad and Mom recalling them many years subsequent.

Not too many miles further on west we encountered remnants of the famous *Bypass Santa Fe Trail*. This part of the Santa Fe Trail was called the "Bypass" because the competitive nature of the competing freight carriers using the trail needed a shorter way to Santa Fe in order to cut off as much time as possible in order to increase their profits. So one of the freight wagon caravans established a new trail going directly southwest from Cimarron, Kansas across the very dry prairie toward Santa Fe. It joined the original Santa Fe Trail at Springer, New Mexico. This proved to be a very big time saver, but the scarcity of water made it necessary to carry an ample supply with the wagon caravan. The Santa Fe Trail was a major trade route to the southwest up until the Santa Fe railroad was built in the late 1870s.

Also, the remnants of the famous Abilene cattle drive trails were crossed. This western country was very flat and chock full of history and places of interest which Mom and Dad constantly discussed in later years, and, of course, they would ask me, "Don't you remember seeing that?" It sort of bothered me to have them ask me those things because I figured they should be able to figure out that I was too young at age two to remember such detail. But, I do appreciate the idea that they were proud of me and just had the idea that I should remember because I was their son. Hmmmmm, parents!! Time passed, the Ford performed beautifully, and we proceeded onward to our new home.

In later years, I retraced that same route as near as possible, and found the new highway follows the old dirt road (which is still visible) very closely all the way to Tucumcari, New Mexico. Of course, today the road is straight and paved and a pleasure to drive upon, and the same trip can be easily made in a day. Most everything has changed during the past seventy four years out west, but some things have not. Those being our memories of the past when we were growing up.

"Of course, Grandma and Grandpa Easley were tickled to death to see us drive up to their place," Mom recalled. Automobiles were quite rare in those parts in the middle twenties, so when our Ford came to a stop, Dad said that his folks both, who had already heard it approaching from a mile away, said their hellos and gave us our hugs, then proceeded to circle the vehicle to inspect every detail. They had food prepared and beds for us to bed down and rest from the long trip. After a couple of days of rest and visiting, Grandpa Jim and Dad left with a wagon and team to inspect the section of land they had selected for Dad to prove up on.

The next several days were spent contacting the rancher who owned a nearby ranch headquarters place which was unoccupied. The permission was obtained and we moved into the place temporarily so Dad could begin building our new home. This allowed Dad to haul the household items the 45 miles out from the train depot at Mountainair and store them at the headquarters. Among those items was Mom's very precious piano and her grandmother's beautiful, fragile, valuable set of Haviland bone-chinaware her grandfather Gottfried Malleis had purchased in Germany in 1886 for Mom's grandmother. I still possess this chinaware.

Of course, there were many other items of value which they wanted to protect, such as carpets, curtains, silverware, chairs, an Edison phonograph, electric lights and the bulbs, electric sweeper, and all those electrical items which were completely useless on the homestead! No electricity existed within 45 miles in any direction. It would be many years until this luxury would come into the area with the advent of the Rural Electrification Administration (REA). These items were carefully re-packed and stored permanently in boxes hoping somehow that by some quirk of fate that electricity would be made available by installing a generator someday; a dream that never materialized due to lack of money.

Rubber garden hoses were another item they brought along, but there was no such thing as *running water*. They were to be used, instead, by cutting them into shorter lengths for siphoning gasoline from the gas barrels into the machinery and for siphoning water from the water barrels on the wagon into the animals' drinking troughs. However, Dad did have plans for such conveniences though. He wanted to construct a wooden tower with a platform on top on which a water storage tank was to be placed. This would provide the height necessary to provide the pressure needed for the running water into the house. The only thing was that the only water available would be the rain runoff from the roof of the house. This would be fine. Dad planned to also place a pump in the system to draw water from the cistern that he would dig at the end of the house which would receive the roof runoff through a charcoal filter to purify the water. Dad had it all designed in his mind.

But the truth was that, in reality, some of his ideas never came into fruition. We would continue to use the water from the cistern, by drawing it up with a bucket on a rope and pulley; the generator was never to become a reality. The *bathroom* would become a storage room for groceries.

CHAPTER 3

* * *

SETTLING IN

The late spring air in central New Mexico was still cold when Dad left to drive the three miles to the homestead to begin his day of work on our new house. We were living in the old sheep ranch headquarters house of the old Jackson Ranch which was located two miles to the north west of our place, the only place available, or for that matter, one of the only vacant houses that existed anywhere nearby in 1926. The only other houses around there were the headquarters ranch house of the old Hester sheep ranch two miles east from our place, and the half-century-old rock ranch headquarters house that joined our place to the east. However, this rock house was occupied by its current owner, Frank Means and his wife Bessie. This Means place did have a good well equipped with a twenty--foot-wheel wooden Eclipse windmill. It was to be one of our main sources of water during the years to come.

Bessie, Mrs. Means, as us boys were instructed to call her, was at the time the only accredited school teacher in the entire area and taught at all the area schools over the ensuing years, including Gran Quivera and Mountainaire and Claunch. She was very tall and of very thin stature, but a very sweet and educated lady of culture. Dad used to tell us in later years that we had to look twice at her shadow in order to see it because she was so thin. Of course, us kids believed everything Dad told us and actually studied her shadow to see if we could see it.

The countryside was so beautiful, those grassy plains with the pine-covered Gallenas Mountains to the east over which the breath-taking seasons' sunrises occurred each morning. Even to this day I have never observed a more beautiful sunrise than those where the sky is always so dark blue and crystal clear with the bright stars of the western sky yielding to the newborn rays of the morning sun.

The "places" as the 640-acre sections were called, were all the same size...one mile square. That made the homesteaders live about a mile apart, or maybe more or less, depending on which side of their place they had their house. So our house was to be located on the south boundary a third of the distance down from the south west corner of Section 23. Dad later said he had figured that the south boundary would be the section line where the state would build a public road some day in the future. As it turned out in later years, he was exactly correct, as he usually always was.

As days passed, the excavated dirt accrued that had been removed by a horse drawn dirt moving machine, known as a *frezno,* until a hole in the ground resulted that was large enough to provide a full basement. Then the arduous work laying the huge limestone rocks, that Dad and a neighbor had quarried some distance away. These would form the basement walls and the house foundation. Weeks passed and the heavy work was finished. Alas! We had a foundation...AND a basement! The basement floor was deliberately left "natural dirt". This was fine because no surface water existed in that part of the country, so there were no springs to be concerned about leaking into the basement as was the case in Kansas. The next concern was obtaining the necessary lumber to begin the actual construction of the house itself.

The Gallinas Mountains (refer to the Map of Central New Mexico Above) were situated about seven miles to the east where Mr. John Morrow, the father of one of our neighbors, had his sawmill set up on U. S. Forest Service land and had a permit to cut the beautiful tall ponderosa pine timber and saw it into lumber for sale. (The word gallinas is a Spanish word which means "chickens" and is pronounced "guy-een-us". The mountain supported, and still does, many wild turkeys, hence its name.) These trees were large virgin timber whose diameter at breast height (referred to by Foresters as DBH) was usually two feet to three feet and stood two to three logs high (a log being 16 feet). The lumber sawn from these trees was of highest quality and usually had no knots in a sixteen-foot length of 1 by 12-inch lumber. This was called "clear select" lumber. These trees were destined to be all harvested by money-hungry loggers during the years to follow. Nowadays, no "clear select" lumber is to be had anywhere due to the greed of a few huge lumber companies and the failure to follow good forest management practices for "sustained yield" of the once-plentiful ponderosa pine timber. Since good roads were non-existent, the only road to the sawmill was one where wagons had made tracks through the prairie and over the hills and into the beautiful mountains and up the canyons to the sawmill. This provided a way into the mill. No large loads, however, could be hauled out because of the rough and rocky condition of the wagon road. So Dad began making the eleven-mile trek to the sawmill and back with perhaps only 300 board feet of rough-sawn lumber on each load. Many trips during the first summer were made until at last he had enough lumber to build the new house from that newly sawed rough lumber. In later years, I remember Dad saying that the price of that lumber was fifteen dollars per thousand board feet. What a contrast to current prices of much lower grades of lumber.

Dad would leave early each morning and drive his wagon and team the three miles to our homestead to do his daily work on the house in order to get it prepared for the family to move into before winter would arrive.

Our Homestead home as it was in 1929.

Usually, cold weather started in October, but snow could come any time after the middle of September. But it was summer time and Mom and I were left alone at the headquarters ranch house.

Mom told of the frightening experience that occurred one day while I was outside playing near the house. She told of the large white hog, which Dad had appropriated for "winter meat," getting out of its pen and decided that I had to be its next meal. I was very small, of course, and couldn't run very fast to escape the oncoming *huge* animal. She heard me screaming and screaming and took a look outside and saw my plight right away. But what could she do? She, being a lady from the "city" had absolutely no idea how to deal with a hog on the loose. But she did what instinct dictated. She took her home-made broom and took after that hog, chased it away from me, and ran it right out of the yard and across the pasture. I suppose I owe my very life to her for her bravery that day there in that yard. Yes, I really do! I discovered later that hogs DO for a fact attack children and do kill them. Also, they DO bite adults, if provoked, or if one tries to interfere with their food source. So country kids do owe more than they realize to their parents, and in a much different way than do city children. Those are two different worlds!

My brother, Don, was born on July 21, 1926. For that big event, Dad and Grandpa Malleis thought it best to send Mom and me back to Newton by train to stay with Mom's cousin on their wheat farm near the town of Hesston until the arrival of the baby. I was a bit over two, then. I remember with some detail that summer there on the farm and the meals at the huge table where all the hired hands ate their noon dinner. I remember the hired hands would tease me about my new brother to be. Of course, I had little understanding of what they were talking about and would remain very quiet and shy. But even more, I remember riding with my cousin, Verna (who I called "Nerna"), into Heston in their Model T Ford to get ice for the lemonade which they made for the hands. I remember I really loved "Nerna", an older teenager. But to me she seemed like an old lady, so tall and big, but we were the greatest of friends and went everywhere together. I became very ingrained in my newly discovered life, and I was told later that I really wanted to stay there forever. I truly loved that farm. Whether or not that experience affected my later desire to own a wheat farm when I grew up, I do not know. But then, came the surprise of my life.

I was totally involved in playing near the edge of the field behind where the parked Model T was, when I heard a voice calling my name. When I responded, I was told to come into the house. "Hurry up," the voice said. So I remember running as fast as my little legs would carry me just to be shown this tiny baby being held by my mother who had disappeared some few days previous. But truthfully, I don't think I really missed her because I was constantly with Nerna. The little baby Mom was holding turned out to be someone Mom called my brother and that he would be going home to New Mexico with us when we returned on the train.

Of course, I just remember parts of all this, but Mom told of the event years later and related how it was that I did not know right off how to deal with the new brother situation, nor could I understand just *why* I had *ran* to the house anyway. I never did understand just what was so important that I had to quit playing and run all the way to the house! But I am sure it went well because I can't remember any serious events of anger or serious battle that made themselves indelible in my memory.

But the time had arrived for our growing family to return to our New Mexico homestead and our father. So Grandpa Ferd Malleis made the arrangements for our things to be transported to the train depot in Newton where he had purchased our tickets for the trip back home. Also, I suppose he slipped a few dollars into Mom's purse while he was at it, because a few new things began to happen once we arrived home...a Fordson tractor? A Model "TT" Ford truck? Finished the house?

The Santa Fe Railway in those days ran several passenger trains each day on its main line which came through Newton. This was the main servicing terminal for the trains and general shops for the locomotives. Also, new train crews boarded the trains for their respective journeys in all directions from Newton. So it was no problem arranging rail travel, no reservations, no future planning, just board the train you preferred and enjoy the trip. Mom took us boys aboard a Pullman train equipped with express and mail cars which stopped only at certain key towns. This made it possible to travel the 600 miles in short order and took only about fifteen hours.

Forrest, 30 Months: Don, 7 Months, 1926.

As our train pulled into the station at Mountainair, Dad was waiting at the depot. Of course, Dad being the well-traveled person that he was, had listened to the telegraph sounder at the telegrapher's desk and knew already the train was due at that particular time. Locomotive engineers prided themselves in being absolutely on time at all destinations. This was no exception. The train pulled in exactly on schedule and Dad was no less punctual. Mom said later that he was very anxious to see his new son and longed to be reunited with his family. I suppose it had been a long lonely summer for him alone there on the homestead working on the new house.

Dad had traded the Model T Ford coupe for a more practical and useful vehicle which he could use on the homestead...a Model TT Ford truck. So our return trip from the train depot to the farm was made no more comfortable by riding in this vehicle which was not known for its luxurious ride. Nevertheless, we arrived home and settled in, according to Mom's recollection, to a life quite different and much more difficult than the one she had quickly become used to during the summer just past.

The house was nearing completion, at least as far as Dad could go with the money he had saved for that purpose. However, additional materials were obtained as additional funds slowly became available from odd jobs and gifts from Grandpa Malleis, so work did progress on the house, and we gained a new neighbor.

The "section" of land which joined our place on the west was homesteaded by a bachelor named Charles Abrams. He was a very neighborly sort and friendly. His mode of transportation was either by horse and wagon or by foot. Usually he walked everywhere he went except, of course, if he had to haul something, he would use his wagon. Now, Mr. Abrams, in his sixties, was a very interesting gentleman. He was a very neat housekeeper, and always kept his chores attended. But the thing I remembered most was that he could sit by the hour and tell the most interesting stories which kept us kids spellbound and laughing. His stories were always so interesting and well-articulated that Mom and Dad found themselves sitting beside us kids totally engrossed. Such entertainment, those story tellers of the past. He had moved from somewhere in the east, but no one knew exactly from where. We all supposed that he came from Kentucky because he would speak of relatives there. He had a daughter who would write to him occasionally which he would tell us about. However, I can't remember her ever coming to visit him. But he would tell us stories of his family when the weather was too bad to be out doors, and on cold days we would all congregate around the wood stove and either exchange stories of the past, or the older folks would discuss plans for the future.

The distance from his one room homestead cabin to our house was about three quarters of a mile which he walked almost every day. Sometimes, he would come over to help in the fields when, actually, he should have been at home working in his own fields. But he was a nice man and a good neighbor and totally unselfish. Of course Dad would go up to his place to return the favors, too. I think Mr. Abrams made the trek by design sometimes, though, because he truly loved Mom's pinto beans and cornbread with the freshly churned butter and buttermilk from our jersey cow. I can't say I blamed him though, looking back, because the very thought of it brings wonderful memories and makes my mouth water even now.

He came to be nicknamed "Hungry". The folks would call him that because it seemed to us that he was always asking for Mom's cooking. But, also, I remembered the times he would walk down to our house to have Dad cut his hair and give him a shave. He bragged that Dad gave the best haircuts and shaves he had ever had in his life. Hungry would always ask me to get up in his lap and pick the blackheads out of his neck. I always thought that was a special thing and enjoyed him asking me to do it. I always thought Hungry was a very special old man because he was so nice to me. He would give me a penny for picking his blackheads. What memories!

To Dad's embarrassment, money kept arriving in the mail from Grandpa Malleis. Grandpa Malleis had served his apprenticeship as a shoe maker in Prussia during his young years prior to his immigration to America. So soon after he arrived in Kansas at age seventeen, he established himself as a shoemaker in his own shop, and over the years that followed he built a very successful business. He could afford to send a few dollars occasionally to Mom and Dad to help out on the farm's expenses. But Dad felt that he himself should support his own family, but in truth, was also grateful for the help from Grandpa. As time passed, Dad purchased a used Fordson tractor and plow to break the virgin sod with and create the field where he would plant his crops of pinto beans and corn and sorghum. The first crop year, 1927, was, as expected, a very non-productive crop year because the newly plowed ground would not produce. In fact, it took another two years of continued plowing and planting and cultivating to get the soil conditioned to support and produce a profitable crop. At the end of the crop year of 1927, which was about November, Dad decided to move temporarily to Albuquerque for the following year to work again at barbering in a first class barber shop (the Sunshine Barber Shoppe) in order to earn enough money to finance another crop and make more improvements to the place. So he rented the farm to a Mr. Dan Addison and his wife who lived there and took care of the place and farmed it on the "shares" during 1928. By the beginning of crop year 1929, they moved back to the homestead and managed to put in a good crop of beans and corn and sorghum. This crop did very well and the rains came when needed and the harvest was bountiful. It was one of the most profitable crop years in history for that area. Dad used to tell of the large yields and good prices he received. I have heard him tell others, "Why, we made twenty sacks to the acre in '29. (A sack being 100 pounds of pinto beans.) That is excellent productivity on a dry farm with no fertilization and irrigation, even today! But Dad realized it wasn't he who had the talent, but God who sent the rains.

In the Easley clan, it was Grandpa Jim who glowed with the farming talents. Grandma was the equal master when it came to the chickens and canning of food for the larder for the future. Each year she had Grandpa sow millet seed in a special seven-acre patch just for her.

The millet was planted because Grandma "ordered" him to so she would have fine grain for her chickens to eat, and she would also have the millet straw for the chickens to scratch in and for her to use to make nests. Grandma had become very successful with her chickens and, by the early thirties, she managed to be selling around sixty dozen eggs or so each week to stores in Mountainair. This, however, presented a real transportation problem because Grandpa Jim could not drive a car and had to depend on neighbors and relatives to drive his 1927 Chevrolet sedan to take the eggs the 45 miles into town each week. This extra income from the chickens was, however, a lifesaver in those years because money was almost nonexistent and one had to be a real manager and planner and a very energetic person full of drive to keep financially afloat.

Many homesteaders failed and had to sell out to neighbors and leave the area. Even Grandpa bought one of the places, the Crowley place, that joined him on the south. With this acquisition, he then owned two sections of land. Mr. Crowley had been working in his field with his team of horses and cultivator during that terribly hot summer when he fell victim to sun stroke. There was vascular hemorrhaging in the brain which resulted in him being partially paralyzed and could no longer care for his place and had to sell it. With this new acquisition, Grandpa Jim was caught in another bind. He had too many acres to farm, more than he could handle single handedly. So he sent for his nephew in

East Texas, Valker Easley, to come to his aid. Valker had been wanting to leave the eastern Texas humidity and hot weather anyway, so he immediately cut all ties there and moved to join Grandpa on his farm. This proved to be a wise arrangement and worked out very well for all concerned, AND we all got to meet a new cousin.

Valker, Grandpa, Grandma Easley By Her Flower Garden (1932).

Valker was a very tall young man in his thirties, I'd guess, and enjoyed working. Also, he was quite experienced in the ways of farm life and had learned to master most jobs required of him. He was a natural in the handling of the farm animals which pleased Grandpa Jim no end, since he himself was a great friend to all his animals and treated them with love and respect. Grandpa could get more work from his mules on a plow or wagon than any man in the area, and all his neighboring farmer friends acclaimed him as the kindest man in the land. With the arrival of Valker on the scene, there was no interruption in the handling of farm animals. This was a big problem during the times before farm tractors made their appearance; hiring of farm hands and continuity of kindness to the animals had to go hand in hand. No good farmer would tolerate their animals being mistreated.

Grandpa's mules were named Jake and Jack and Jenny. We had a white mule named Toby, and when either Grandpa or we needed a four-up team of mules, we would hitch the four together abreast into a team. At this point in this writing it becomes necessary to iterate that a four-up team of mules is not to be considered the same as a four-up team of horses, no way!! Any driver who has experience with both of these teams knows for a fact that a mule can outwork any horse and that a mule's memory exceeds his lifetime for sure, or at least, it would seem that way. No mule, in addition to being very stubborn, would ever forget being mistreated or loved, and, moreover, they remember WHO did it! They seem to hold a grudge for ever and ever. AMEN.

An example of this goes back to an experience I had with a two-up team of mules. I was plowing with a go-devil (a one-row sled with knives on the sides and disks on the rear with a seat for the driver). To hasten one of the mules who had dropped back a bit, I popped him with the end of the lines and he jumped back into position and all was well...I thought! The next morning when I was rounding up the horses and mules in the pasture to bring them into the corral to harness them for work, this mule decided to get even. And get even he tried! He came alongside the horse I was riding and turned ninety degrees to the horse and raised his rear end into the air and kicked both his rear feet extremely hard at me. I was a very lucky boy that he missed. Yep! He missed my leg and kicked the horse I was riding bareback in the side, resounding as would a tenor drum, darn near knocking over my mount which would have dumped me on the ground. I don't know whether one has *lucky stars*, but I thanked them anyway for I could have ended up with two broken legs that day! From that time on, I used great care in working any mule that I had occasion to use, and I was always very careful not to do anything to antagonize it for fear of some sort of retaliation.

Grandpa Jim, however, had no problems with any of his animals except for one strawberry roan mare of his. The mules all loved Grandpa,

I imagine because he pampered them by hand feeding them grain as and patting them on the cheek and talking some sort of special language only he and the mules understood. Never did they ever turn on him. But Dad wasn't so gentle to animals, nor did he talk baby talk to them, nor did he pet them. His was a world of work and he expected the animals to perform accordingly. Little wonder the animals were on their guard and vindictive, so to speak, at our house. Now, that strawberry roan mare was another story!

This young roan mare hated to conform! She hated to work! She hated to be harnessed into a team! So Grandpa would blindfold her with a gunny sack over her face so she couldn't see what was taking place around her. He, then, was able to harness her and get her hooked to a plow or wagon. As I iterated, she hated work and being driven, and most of the time at her first opportunity such as Grandpa turning at the end of the row, that mare would absolutely go out of her ever-lovin' mind and begin to run in a hard lope across the field taking the plow and the rest of the team with her! Such a sight! Grandpa usually managed to hang on and remain seated on the plow, for a while, at least. But eventually, he would get bounced off and land in the midst of his crop on the posterior part of his overalls. His well-worn old floppy gray felt hat and his plug of *Brown Mule* chewing tobacco, which he always carried in his right front pocket, would become airborne and become the objects of an eventual careful search of the area.

We kids liked to visit the grandparents often and would be around the house with Grandma, and, per chance, would witness this type of event. We thought it a very hilarious happening, that is until Grandma caught us laughing. The sever scolding we would get quickly imprinted upon our immature young minds that we just didn't "...laugh at Grandpa!"

The horses would eventually wind up running until they ran into the fence corner and stop, and the sweat from their soaking-wet hides and the white froth from their mouths would drip to the ground. Grandpa would just let them stand there a while until they would get over their fit, then he would walk across the field and retrieve his team and continue his plowing. The wild roan mare, by then, usually would be worn down and would settle-in to her role in the team. Such is breaking a wild horse to work, and Grandpa was the best!

CHAPTER 4
* * *
THE GREAT DEPRESSION

It seemed that the great depression which was said to have started in 1929, certainly didn't apply to our part of the country. The truth is that the economy and life style of the western states was so poor in those days that there was little difference in times before the depression started and after it started. The major difference was that the year of 1929 was a very good year for crops in our part of the country, and yields were high, and selling prices were high. In fact, we never suffered from the depression at all except that the following year, the best I remember, banks were closed and prices of goods were rock bottom. But that didn't affect Dad in the least because he didn't use the banks anyway. He didn't trust them at all, nor did many others in the area. He kept his money at home and guarded it with a rifle and shotgun (which I still possess). Most everyone in the area did the same. The thing that bothered Dad the most was when President Franklin Roosevelt called in all the gold coins that were in circulation. Dad had a few, but ones he held as coins he would keep for security purposes and then to hand down to his children. One of his great qualities was that he expected everyone to obey the law. So when this law was passed, he dutifully returned the coins to the nearest bank the first chance he got. What made him really mad was when he found out the banker was a coin collector (they still are) and had "collected" the gold coins returned by him. So at that point in his life Dad decided that since things were so dishonest in banks and in business, and in the government and related agencies, that the next time a similar law was passed, he simply would destroy the item

instead of "turning it in" as the law required. The same was true when
the Congress proposed to "register" all guns in 1936. Dad destroyed
his revolver because he figured it would get into the wrong hands and
some "businessman" would use it for profit of some kind. Those were
interesting times, too, because money lenders were bent on foreclosing
and taking land away from the land owners for the slightest infraction
in the payment of loans. We had observed on so many occasions the
lenders, usually local banks, taking one's land and other property in
foreclosure just to gain title to the property, then rent or lease it back to
the owner for a percentage of the yield of the crop. This practice was a
huge business and widely practiced, and I understand it still is. So this
forced the farmers into a corner because they did not want the banks
to obtain their land under any circumstances. As a result, the farmers
adopted a new approach to money lenders. The new practice that the
people were forced into by the banks' dishonesty was that if one didn't
have the money to pay for a thing, they didn't need the item no matter
what it was. The new method (actually an "old" method revived) of
paying for an item if one didn't have money to pay for it was to trade
the products from your labors, other than money, for the item. This cut
the banks out of the picture all together and eliminated the problem of
foreclosure. The farmers and ranchers never were much for investing in
the stock market, so that wasn't the reason for them to withdraw their
money from the banks, as the papers had stated. The real reason was
the farmers came to not trust the dishonest banks and withdrew their
money and took it home with them where they kept personal charge
of it on their own premises, thus, again, cutting out the bank from the
loop. They didn't like the whole idea of the banks "using" their money
to reap high interest profits for themselves and only pay the depositor
a measly interest rate for the "use" of their hard-earned money. Also,
they, during that time of financial unrest in the country, didn't trust
the banks' wisdom in investing the farmers' money and were afraid the
banks would lose it, which most of them did. So to get around all the
whole mess of dishonesty and greed and bad investment strategies, the
farmers around there just refused to do business with the banks at all,
thus forcing them to close down. So there are more ***real*** reasons than

just the "stock-market crash" that closed the banks, at least in our part of the country.

When tractors became a common item on the farm in the area, the store keepers usually held the account open for the gas and oil and grease to operate them until harvest time in the fall of the year. At that time, the farmers would pay up for the full year's expense. No interest was charged and the only profit for an item was the standard markup set for the item. The standardized markup percentages were common. For example, two to four percent markup for canned grocery items, 40 percent for hardware items, two cents per gallon for gasoline (which sold for eleven cents) and 100 percent for luxury items such as jewelry, and so on. Also, for a person or store to charge interest on unpaid balances, they had to be licensed as a "lending agency" as well. Haven't things changed? I sometimes wonder whether the laws have actually been modified to allow for everyone to charge interest, or whether the law looks the other way because of the fear of lobbyists. Also, customized profit margins have disappeared too, haven't they? In addition, one could drive to Detroit and buy a new car without violating the dealer's "franchise" and not pay the dealer's markup when buying the car at the factory. People used to do that to save the markup, the freight, and they would get a vacation out of the deal to boot. (The last person I knew who did that was a friend in Boulder, Colorado who drove to Detroit and picked up a new Oldsmobile Rocket 88 in 1953.)

But, back to the depression years. There weren't only the economic problems at hand for most of us, but there was the weather which was a major player. Yes, the weather had changed as well. Drought conditions swept the country and rain was as scarce as money, or even more scarce in some areas. The dust bowl, centered in New Mexico, West Texas, Colorado and Kansas, was partially amplified by neophyte people coming out west and trying their hand at farming, but those newcomers were all trying to "make it" in a place in which none of them was familiar. The weather was the other big cause. Those new and inexperienced "farmers" merely "scratched" the eluvium of the west, as they did the heavy clay loam soil in the east, which allowed the hot winds to further dry it out and blow it away and create huge dunes. Also, huge clouds of sky borne soil particles filled the windy atmosphere and traveled all the way to the Mississippi valley and even further before settling back to the surface of the earth.

The experienced farmer of the west, on the other hand, hardly had that problem because he plowed very deeply and formed a soil texture of "clods" which were wind resistant and did not blow. Also, this course texture served to collect the drifting sand from other farms and helped stabilize the soil to keep it from getting airborne. Even the County Farm Agents circulated bulletins instructing farmers to plow deeply and form a "textured" soil to prevent erosion. The farmers were instructed to plant crops in "strips" to form barriers to retain the soil and interrupt the wind currents. Also, wind breaks and barriers of Chinese elm trees were planted which helped. However, the problem did not resolve itself until after people had sold their places to ranchers and left the area. They, most of them, went to the war plants of California and the Oregon and Washington ship yards. This part of the "story" of the dust bowl one rarely reads about in history books, papers, magazine articles, or technical essays. Nevertheless, that is what happened with me as an eye witness.

The ranchers, of course, were not interested in farming, so they let the grass grow back, since it was the climax plant of the area, and they used it to graze their cattle. As a result, the dust storms disappeared for the most part and only the wind was left. The grass roots held the soil and made it stable once more. But those were interesting times, times which taught us many things about survival and living harmoniously; survivors we were! Other farmers chose to remain in the state, but accepted offers of federal money to let the fields lay idle and unfarmed. Most of those farms still receive those funds and the farms are still idle, thus keeping farm produce surpluses at a minimum and keeping the retail prices high for the same items.

Also, we never heard of a "bread line", except in the newspaper. Nor did we hear of being "jobless". There was always work to be had, and there was work to be done on the farm by those who wanted it and were not too lazy to do it. The farm always rewarded one with food of some kind and a place to protect one from the elements. But we did understand the situation of others living in the cities where they could not raise their own food nor provide for themselves on their own places.

Just as it has always been in the cities throughout history, people were totally dependent upon someone else. We grew up to be humble about our blessings and to share them with those who weren't so blessed. And for those who had not, we managed to arrange a trade of some kind. We were careful not to embarrass them with a gift, but to let them "earn" it with labor. Actually, money wasn't usually needed.

But most trading was done by bartering anyway, so money didn't play much of a role in our local economy. I remember salesmen would come around selling their wares which varied from fruit to used cars, to new cars, to sewing machines, to groceries, to shoes, to clothing, to books, to whatever you could imagine. Even men came around during colder weather selling butchered pork and beef. Of course no one had what we now refer to as refrigeration or refrigerators or ice boxes. No ice was available nor did it exist anywhere outside the large towns during the warmer months. When we butchered our own pork and beef, we would wait until the cold weather arrived in November, then hang it on the north side of the house to freeze. We would rub it down with black pepper to keep the flies off and wrap it with white cloth to keep dust off. But if we in the community would have traded for these items, we would have traded cows or horses or chickens or hogs or sacks of pinto beans or sacks of shelled corn or jars and buckets of molasses or whatever else we had to trade. In fact, looking back, I believe those were the most enjoyable and the most sensible and peaceful days of my life. Cheating people and "ripping off" people were unheard of until I moved to the city many years later. A cheater would either have been blackballed by the rest of the community or been punished directly by the victim and, as a result, would have suffered for his transgressions many times over. Here's an example of how the "law" worked "out west". (By the way, it still is this way out west in several locations!)

The cattle ranch to our north comprised 120 deeded sections of land and about 50 sections of permitted land from the U.S. Forest Service. It was owned by the Atkinson family, Marshal, his wife, and son Joe. Joe was a grown man and the son of Marshal's brother who had been married to Mrs. Atkinson but passed away as the result of an alleged ambush when Joe was a teenager. Marshal married Joe's mother and started helping run the ranch which had proved too much for Joe and his mother alone. Together, they prospered and the ranch grew and eventually they were running about a thousand head of Hereford cattle. The pastures in that area support a sustained heard of five and a half cows per section of land (640 acres). So during bad years for farming, some folks, for one reason or another, would be in desperate need of food. This one family, I remember, (won't mention their names) weren't the best of farmers in the world, and usually didn't raise much on their neglected fields and came to the point they actually had no food on their table. Their crop hadn't receive the rains it needed and help just wasn't there. So in an effort to help the situation, their oldest son, who was in his middle twenties, got into his old rattle-trap pickup truck and drove into the edge of the Atkinson ranch which was adjacent to a graded country road. He stopped at a place where he had spotted a few cows grazing and got out of the truck carrying his 22-caliber rifle and situated himself in firing range to kill one of the cows in order to provide food for the family at home. He shot a cow using this small rifle which he figured couldn't be heard very far, and then proceeded to butcher and quarter the beef and load it onto his truck.

What he failed to realize was that almost all ranchers out west are armed Deputy Sheriffs. And those who aren't deputized carry weapons on their ranches anyway, AND WILL USE THEM!! Well, as one can guess, Joe just happened to be riding that part of the range, as he did quite regularly, and had heard the old pickup coming down the road and stop. His curiosity was aroused, so he took out his binoculars and watched the entire operation. Actually, Joe recognized the cattle thief as the son of the local farmer. So without a second thought, Joe got onto his horse and rode over to confront the thief and arrested him on the spot with the evidence in his hand, so to speak. As it turned out, Joe was a very warm hearted and considerate person and allowed the beef to be taken on home by the young man to the needy family. BUT he did deliver the thief to the county jail and took him to immediate trial for stealing and killing a cow. He asked the judge to have mercy on the family and give him only the minimum sentence for a felony...stealing a cow. This was a year and a day in the New Mexico State Penitentiary. It was granted! The time was served, no parole, no anything, just hard prison time at hard labor. Needless to say, that was the end of his lawlessness. He did learn how to work during his stay in the pen, and after he was released, he secured a good job on a farm and the family made a complete turnaround. His brother, Tod, became an installation representative for steel buildings in that area, and became quite successful.

But one could get SHOT out west trespassing on another's property, especially on a cattle ranch. Those cattle and sheep ranches were and are very large (usually over a hundred sections) and were and are privately owned, and inaccessible and off limits to the public, and to most lawmen. It's a matter of conjecture of the amount of time which could elapse before a skeleton would be discovered, if ever, thereon. May stories are told for the truth of certain individuals, including lawmen, who have totally disappeared never to be heard from again. I have no doubt, having been raised there, of the validity of most of those stories.

The work days were long whether during winter or during spring plowing or during summer cultivation of the young crop plants in the fields or during harvest time and gathering and threshing of the crops. Our days usually started, for most folks, about four a.m. with the sound of a very loud alarm clock strategically placed by the head of the house. One of our neighbors, Finis Jones, for example, placed his Big Ben windup alarm on a dishpan under his bed. I remember when I stayed overnight at his house as a guest when I was barely a teenager and thought the very world had exploded when that terrible clock decided to do its thing. It was in the dead of winter time and Finis had been off running his trap line, which in total was about sixty miles long, for about three weeks and had Desmond Winters, my class mate, staying there to care for the animals and keep the ice broken on their drinking water buckets and barrels. So we had set the alarm as Finis had instructed. That night was miserably cold and windy and snowing hard. We all piled into the same double bed, onto which were placed five or six heavy quilts, in order to keep warm. We were very tired as usual and fell asleep right away. Then...RRRRRIIIINNNNNGGGGGGGGGG!!

We simultaneously jumped right out of our skins. I had NEVER heard such a loud alarm in my life. I told Desmond that I would never,

ever spend another night with him there! But I did. We laughed about it a little, then managed to get our feet out from under those warm quilts and onto that very frozen wood floor and into our clothes. It should be noted here that we slept with our shoes and folded clothes placed at our feet inside the covers. But you can bet we scurried to the stove and built a roaring fire in it as soon as we could get over to it. And so it was, during those winters on the homesteads where the elevation was nearly 7,000 feet above sea level, and the temperatures were proportional.

In those days in that area, keeping a fire going at night was near impossible. First, the wood of the area that was available to burn in the heating stove was pinyon pine and had to be hauled by wagon for miles from the foothills. Also, it burned hot and fast, so one would have had to get out of bed every couple of hours to refill the stove. Also, that meant one would have to chop, with an axe, much more wood to last the night. So it certainly made more sense to just put more quilts on the beds and cover up your heads and just let your noses stick out to keep from suffocating.

Quite often, I would spend the night with Desmond and help him do the chores, then we would have to walk the mile and a half back to our house by seven a.m. to catch the school bus in front of our house. Of course, we had already fixed and eaten our bacon and eggs or sausage or hot cakes prior to leaving Finis's house.

Sometimes Don, my younger brother, would accompany me to Finis's house and share in the chores and cooking and walking back the next morning. Mom, however, figured that he, being only about ten years old, probably shouldn't be exposed to walking in the snow on those cold mornings which usually dipped to near zero degrees which forced us to wrap up in our old tattered hand-me-down coats from relatives and friends in Kansas. She was, of course, right as always. Don usually was prone to catching a cold or something before the rest of us would.

We had no "overshoes," as we referred to them. We wore our work shoes which Dad had coated many times over with tallow which we always saved after butchering a beef. The tallowed shoe was held close to the hot wood stove to melt the tallow into the leather, thus making it water proof which kept our feet dry and warm when walking through the drifted snow. The cold didn't seem to affect us that much, but as one can figure out, we were "country wise" and quite able and knowledgeable to survive most every difficult situation placed in our path.

Times were hard most everywhere, and in our community there were few exceptions, to that statement. I remember, though, one man in particular. I shall refer to him as "Frank" for purposes of this recollection. Frank had everything he could possibly need or want. He and his wife had built a beautiful new white clapboard home on the west side of the village of Claunch on land he owned there. In fact, he owned all the land in sight to the west and north of his home. He had bought out homesteader folks who had hit hard times and had to sell. Of course, Frank only offered a minimum price for the land he was offered in such instances, usually ten cents to a dollar per acre depending upon the improvements. But his new home included a nice "dining room" and fancy curtains and varnished floors. It also included a beautiful garage for his new car. He always wore a suit of some kind with tie and patent leather shoes. He owned many farms around the countryside which he obtained similarly. Of course, he usually rented those places back to the original owners on shares. This meant that the renter would pay Frank a fourth of the crop at harvest time before expenses were paid by the renter.

Frank never owned a still, or, at least, no one ever said they knew of one under Frank's ownership. However, Frank did deal secretly on Saturday nights in a strong beverage the "T-Men" seemed to stay quite interested in. The grown folks who drank would usually keep the path to Frank's house quite busy, on the sly, of course. Everyone would always say that is how he obtained most of his fortune during prohibition times. Frank was quite a powerful local politician and had quite a pull at the county seat. But Frank had a very warm heart and would lend farmers money to make the next year's crop on a handshake. Of course, foreclosure was also in his vocabulary, but only as a last resort in the event long after (unlike the banks) the farmer could not or would not pay up. Frank did not charge interest as I remember, but he did prefer payment of a portion of the crop so he could speculate on the profits to be obtained by "holding" the crop for higher prices. This was and is the practice of farmers who are well enough off to be able to hold the crop and not have to sell it to pay bills.

Another farmer, whom I shall refer to as Jeff, was also into the bootleg business on the side. Jeff was a bit different by the fact that he had a good still and knew how to operate it. Living out forty five miles from the nearest town was of great benefit when it came to isolation from the law. Jeff was very open with the operation of his moonshine operation and did manage to survive the depression with many amenities not common to a homesteader of the area and the times. One story concerning this fellow I always enjoyed hearing folks tell. I shall repeat it here. It is true and it occurred circa 1930. Only the name is fictitious.

It seems that Jeff learned that country dances were being held on Saturday nights in the *new* Claunch school building that had been recently completed. His mental "wheels" began to turn and it didn't take him long to figure out that he could sell his moonshine there, secretly, of course. Far be it from Jeff to sell it openly at a dance, especially at the new school house, and stand a chance of some visiting lawman spotting him breaking the law. No! Not Jeff! As it happened, Jeff also had a contract with the county to run one of the two contract school buses. Since he owned the school bus himself, he kept it at his farm and used it as he chose during off times. So on Saturday night about the time the dance would begin, Jeff would show up in his school bus loaded with half-gallon fruit jars full of his "creation."

Well! Sales went well! But Jeff was nobody's fool! No, Sir! Jeff did not partake of his most potent alcoholic beverage himself for good reason. He stayed sober in order to remain sharp and watch those who did drink it. This trait paid off handsomely. One thing he did was to stay near his "loaded" school bus for a couple of reasons. One reason was that he didn't trust anyone near the bus and its cargo. The other reason was that he kept a keen eye on those who would buy a jar of moonshine and sneak off around the corner of the school house to have a sip together with either their buddy, their girlfriend, or someone else's wife. When they had finished sipping their fill they would stash the remainder of it under the school house or behind a fence post or somewhere they figured no one could find it. Surprise, surprise! Jeff did!

Jeff, as soon as the fellow would go back inside to the dance, would quietly go over and retrieve the jar. Well, now, Jeff being no idiot, knew the fellow would emerge soon for another sip of his own personal stock that he only recently had purchased, sipped, and hid so well. But, alas! No whiskey! Being a bit inebriated, they would want to fight the first person they encountered for "stealing" their jar and drinking their whiskey. According to one account, two men got into a fight one Saturday night because both their fruit-jars of moonshine were missing from their respective hiding places. The men had encountered each other as they both hunted for their jars. They each accused the other of being a thief and the fight began. These weren't young men, but middle-aged farmers with families. They fought, they wrestled, they hit each other with whatever they could find handy, they cursed each other, and then one got the other down on the ground and proceeded to bite off his nose. Yeah! Clear to his face! The whole end of it! This is a true story and is a matter of court record. Dad was the Justice-of-the-Peace and checked on the story's validity. Mr. Courtney, (not his real name) the one who lost his nose, never had it grafted back on. He chose to let it stay as it was. So I grew up seeing him around the area without the end of his nose; quite strange seeing two holes into his face instead of a nose. Those were the days!

But that isn't the end of the story. Jeff would refill the retrieved fruit jars back to their original level and resell them to the original purchaser. Talk about a business man! This went on until the end of prohibition. No one ever was the wiser, for the ones who knew, had tight lips...of necessity!

Uncle Jess, Dad's brother, was a man of many facets, a man of drive, a man unafraid to try something different for a living. But he was also a good man. He provided for his family well and they always came first in his life. He never to my knowledge ever went to church except, maybe, to an occasional funeral, *and* there is another thing for sure. He had a wonderful wife, Aunt Ethyl.

I shall always remember visiting uncle Jess's house when I was growing up. Deeeeelishus!!!! OH, yes! I am referring to that wonderful home-made ice cream Aunt Ethyl used to make. Yeah! From pure jersey cream, too!! I also remember helping crank that five-gallon ice cream freezer. I think that was the biggest ice cream freezer I have ever seen, even to this day. I remember all the relatives would plan to congregate there and the boys who were big enough to either "hold down" that big freezer or to crank it would be assigned those jobs by Aunt Ethyl, and to the back yard we would all go arguing over who would get to turn the crank on that big flywheel.

Of course, it wouldn't be long after the ice cream began to freeze that the one cranking would start begging someone else to take his place. But, then, when the two boys cranking and the two boys sitting on the freezer could no longer turn the crank and hold down the freezer, we knew our efforts would soon be well rewarded with a huge bowl of the best pure vanilla ice cream in the whole world. Such memories! I truly feel pity for those who never experienced life on the farm during the depression. What a wonderful way to grow up!

Then, there's Aunt Ethyl's southern fried chicken. The chicken that we boys had to chase and catch and help pick those smelly feathers just after Uncle Jess had decapitated it with his trusty double-bit axe.

Then there were all those scrumptious home-made pies AND cakes and home-made jams and jellies all served up on the same Sunday dinner table with that fried chicken and cornbread and all the other trimmings. No these weren't holidays, just Sunday dinners. Mom learned about all she knew about "southern cooking" from Aunt Ethyl, a dear sweet lady whom we all loved dearly.

Uncle Jess was a good farmer by local standards and always managed to have good equipment to farm with. When he spent money, it was usually for necessities for the family, first, then he would invest in a new tractor complete with the implements built for it, a new drilled well and windmill, a new barn that he could store his good wagon and new 1930 Chevrolet truck in out of the weather, and other related farm necessities as needed. But times being like they were, he took on other responsibilities for pay as well. One of these was to provide school bus services for the school.

Uncle Jess went to the Socorro County School Board and argued that another school bus was badly needed for that area he lived in to haul the kids to school. After some consideration, they agreed and contracted with him to provide and run the school bus. That's one of the reasons he purchased the new 1930 Chevrolet truck. He immediately built a body for it to haul the two dozen children. The seats were unpadded benches; one down each interior side of the bus body and one down the center with a bench seat on either side of a central back rest. The entrance and exit were through a rear door in the center. The body was constructed with a wooden floor and a wooden frame work covered with galvanized steel roofing material. Rural school buses like this were built by all the bus providers in the new western communities down through the years of the thirties and served very well the purpose. There was no heat during winter except what heat from the vehicle's cab heater could pass through the rear window of the truck's cab which had been removed and a canvas boot installed instead. In an effort to save a little money, Uncle Jess decided to use "coal oil," (kerosene) as it was called then, in the radiator of the school bus as an anti-freeze coolant since it was so much cheaper than the regular alcohol anti-freeze solution commonly used. However, this decision proved to be a disastrous one. During one of his runs, the engine caught fire from the coal oil leaking onto the hot engine through holes which had been eaten through the radiator hoses by the coal oil. He hadn't known that the coal oil would eat up the rubber hoses. Of course, he had no insurance, and had to purchase another new truck and build another bus body onto it. Experience is a wonderfully difficult "teacher" sometimes.

In the areas of the United States east of New Mexico there were established schools that had better "factory-made" school buses where needed. But the western people had little money and less established industry, so we had to make do with what we could come up with. But I hasten to add that in no way did this hinder the quality of education we received, because the teachers were absolutely dedicated, and didn't let the lack of money affect their work. If something was needed, it was improvised and life went on as is discussed in other parts of this writing. The bus was cold inside, but we just wore our heavy coats and faired quite nicely. Of course, people of today's society are so spoiled and tender that luxurious school buses equipped with the latest heating and air conditioning systems replete with FM radio and video and total freedom to act like an idiot are a requirement of the times.

(AUTHOR'S NOTE: The school board in that part of New Mexico was a board of directors whose responsibility it was to administer and supervise ALL the schools in the very large county, the largest county in the entire country I understand. Socorro County at that time measured some eighty miles wide, north to south, and one hundred ninety miles long, east to west. (It has since been divided into two large counties, Socorro and Catron.) This county comprised many schools in the outlying areas as well as several city schools. Also, it is well to note that there was only one school superintendent to supervise all those school principals and the related business of planning and curriculum. They did well, and I never even dreamed of a school system having more than one superintendent per county until I moved to Missouri. What a huge waste of tax money having a "superintendent for every principal." As a matter of "challenge," I refer the public school systems of any state, who claim that "one" superintendent is inadequate to administer all schools in a sovereign county of a given state, to the Catholic School System of the Springfield-Cape-Girardeau Diocese which encompasses the entire southern third of the state of Missouri. This Catholic School System is administered by ONE Catholic nun as Superintendent. She does a magnificent job and is the envy of every public school administrator in the state. And she does it with absolutely no financial help from the state or federal government or from taxation. It is funded totally by donations, interest on investments, and fund-raising events. It amounts to about one tenth the money of a similar "public" school system using unlimited "tax" money which is raised simply by assessing and re-assessing over and over the real estate valuation and increasing the tax base of real estate and other taxables. *AND*, the quality of education and buildings and equipment is second to none! This is a huge thorn in my side and makes me extremely angry at selfish politicians and school administrators and school board members who are usually untrained in matters of business and education and hiring requirements of "good" and qualified teachers, and management of industrial operations such as a public school. Also, I resent their very stubborn attitude that only "they" are right and are the only "experts" at running schools. They not only forget, but they refuse to remember they "work for" the tax payer and are hired to operate the schools and to educate the children in accord with the wishes of the taxpayer, not the teacher. The states must learn a lesson and learn from the private schools how to manage and operate their schools much better for much less money, and how to better teach the subjects therein.)

The small country schools where I grew up never had the luxury of very much money in their budgets. They made do with what they had and never had the attitude of "having" to have money to teach children. They believed that teaching was mostly the transferring of knowledge and experience from the teacher to the student and supervising and guiding them wisely in attaining the experience level necessary to go into the world of *their* choice, not the teacher's, equipped well enough to live in the style they chose and to have the knowledge to better themselves when the occasion might arise. If money should ever have been required for some necessary purpose, the parents were contacted by the principal and, together, they worked things out on an individual basis. If a new school building were needed, the folks in the surrounding area got together and built it. If an extra teacher were needed, a qualified (high school or better) person in the community volunteered to fill the need until the superintendent could hire one. He would "look" for one, not wait for one to apply. How times have changed!

The school year was established as a nine-month year which began in September and ended in June, having a week off between Christmas and New Year's day. There were no so-called "snow days" to make up nor were "teacher's meetings" held on week days. These were on weekends except for one teacher's convention annually held during only one week in the state capital, Santa Fe. Text book subjects were divided into chapters to be taught each week, and that was uniform and had to be adhered to by all teachers. Also during snow storms during times when roads were impassable and the school buses could not run, the students were given assignments to be done at home in order to keep the flow of the subject in sync with the text and the tests. Parents saw to it that the kids did their homework ahead of chores.

(How different today: NO chores, NO homework, parents who could care less, so sad. Result: complete "freedom," very poor education, irresponsible and irreverent citizens because the young people lose that deeply ingrained mandate to follow obedient and morally upright lives, instead of the desire to be absolutely "free" to do as they please!)

But the impassable roads were quickly opened by the farmers who lived adjacent to the roads, and the county was hardly ever relied upon for clearing roads. If that had been the case, it would have taken weeks for the county machines to travel the 75 miles from Socorro over closed roads to clear ours. So we, the community, cleared our own, usually the same day the snow occurred—no cost to the county either.

Each spring before school was out in June, the teachers planned a picnic trip to the Gallenas Mountains for a day for the entire school. It was truly a picnic! I remember country fried chicken and home-made lemonade and home-made pies and cakes and cookies and sausages and breads and sandwiches of all kinds. I remember oranges too. They and bananas were a very rare treat which we hardly ever saw except when the store keeper, Mr. Spear, ordered them special for just such an occasion, or maybe for Christmas. Fresh lemons were used in the lemonade. I well remember we kids all participated in squeezing them and then dropping the remaining squeezed peelings into the wash-tub-full of lemonade to float and add to the flavor. I still remember that delicious lemonade and am still an avid partaker of the beverage.

The picnic site was in a ponderosa pine timber stand in the Cibola (pronounced "see-bo- la") National Forest in an open meadow covered with soft grass which provided an excellent area for baseball. Of course, the very first thing had to be that all the adults and larger boys lined up across the area and searched it for any existing rattle snakes and killed them. The girls and boys both participated on the same teams and were chosen by who ever got the ball and bat from the truck first. We rode to the mountains in a farmer's one-and-a-half-ton, stake-side truck and the teachers' cars. The road was the same road my father drove his wagon on to haul the lumber to build our house from the sawmill which was nearby the picnic site. This was a beautiful area and very practical, too. There was a nice spring filled with ice-cold water from the melting snow in the upper slopes and was located just a small distance from where all the activity took place. We boys took the responsibility of procuring what water was needed from the spring. The picnic was an annual event and shall always be in the memories of all who participated.

The Depression of the thirties, whatever its cause, brought with it an infinite array of circumstances which resulted in an infinite array of problems, of situations, of relationships, of sorrows, of social changes, and of economic changes all of which resulted in several new societies being born within our own country. New laws were passed, new procedures were adapted in our congress, new interpretations of our constitution were made, strict laws were abolished and new looser laws were passed, and total freedom given by the new Supreme Court, and religion was removed from all public schools at the hand of an atheist, and lobbyists got into control. As a result, we have emerged a much more "free" and chaotic and independent immoral people saturated with crime and disrespect for each other, and an extremely corrupt government, and dishonest businesses, and not to mention totally immoral "entertainment."

Yes, I remember ("before the war" and before the new Supreme Court interpretations) that children and teachers respected God and felt free to discuss and teach His teachings in any classroom or hallway. I remember when all children had total respect for their God and their parents beyond any doubt. People respected their elders, each-others' ages, profession or occupation, and gave them credit for being the experts that they were. I remember that teachers were greatly respected both in and out of the classroom, and that teachers actually practiced in public the good grammar they taught in classes and expected the same of the students and parents. I remember school children holding quasi elections in the classroom on election-day. I remember the children actually took interest in the candidates and checked to see who they liked best for the job, as they could imagine in their own minds and not the minds of their parents. I remember children wanted to read the newspaper and discussing it with adults. I remember the children were taught to read and evaluate and count the ballots with great accuracy. I remember children wanted to look nice in public. I remember girls wanted to be feminine and look the part so boys would like them and respect them as young women, as God's most magnificent creation. I remember when boys wanted girls to respect them as gentlemen, and only the "wild" ones would dare lay a hand on a girl on a date and were considered woman chasers and were not allowed around decent families by the protective fathers. I remember the school principal could and DID whip a child's posterior for disrespect and seriously breaking the rules, then I remember the child's father repeating the punishment for the same infraction when he or she got home from school. I remember children could be and were permanently expelled from school for serious infractions of school rules and the law. Nowadays, parents have the teacher in public schools "fired" for even speaking out to the child. My! How times have been changed by that Court ruling. A good society turned bad. Love and respect turned to independence and disrespect and hatred and indifference and self-centeredness. Yes, I remember these things that I speak of and have both seen and experienced first-hand across the land.

Speaking of memories, the advent of my being allowed to live a long life, long enough to be alive in both the twentieth and the twenty first centuries, year 2001, causes my memory to drift back to the prewar days of the late twenties and the thirties. I speak of this because as I get older, older with years, I can't help but observe the social disintegration of the American families. Specifically, I call everyone's attention to the fact that since the advent of WWII and the advent of the modern transportation, especially the automobile, and the advent of technologically advanced communications and entertainment devices, our family members, especially children, have become scattered about across the nation and world. This has led to the situation where family members hardly know each other or, in most cases, rarely communicate regularly and often. As grand children are born and grow up, they usually don't become close to the grandparents or other relatives such as aunts and uncles.

As my memory drifts back to prewar days, I recall that most families were very, very closely situated geographically and usually visited often and regularly. Everyone had great respect for our country and the military for keeping us safe and secure. This stayed so for most of their lives for the most part. I remember my grandparents on both sides except my mother's mother who passed on to her reward the year prior to my birth. I, as is demonstrated throughout this writing, not only remember my relatives, but was fairly close to them and very close to some, the ones I came in contact with more often. This type of relationship in this new so-called "wonderful 21ˢᵗ century" has disappeared almost totally in that almost every family of parents under fifty years of age is scattered to the four winds because of many modern reasons such as "chosen professions" divorce, personal whims and so on.

Another thing I notice is the fact that there are those "baby boomers" who now have married children who have become scattered across the face of the earth, and the parents try their doggone best to follow them around as they move away from home and from one job to another; just to be "near our children." They just can't cut the umbilical cord it seems, and THAT causes a new problem: they (the baby boomers) destroy the relationship with THEIR parents which happen to still be living and need them more than ever in their old age! Such is the case with so many of our friends and relatives and their families. The sequence of bibliographic information presented thus far, is to exemplify the great downturn of our society during the last sixty years, even though the psychologists and sociologists say we are having a great "progress" in our social relationships. I disagree! Little do THEY know from life's true experience.

I have always contended that the word "progress," as used by almost everyone, is erroneous from the outset. The ones using that term fail to define it for us and fail to present the "basis" for their definition of the term. One MUST state the starting point they use in order to list subsequent events which must be compared to the starting point then referred to the baseline of either morality, immorality, time, or some other meaningful basic reference in order to determine whether one is progressing from one point to another in time, morality, immorality, and so on.

I, personally use the baseline of morality and time to define "progress" as I believe it should be defined, and that is with reference to society existing in accordance with Gods rules and plan, NOT with reference to MAN's desires and pleasures. If, for instance, we proceed from one point on the scale of morality to a lower point on the scale of morality, then the direction of travel through time is called "REgression" not PROgression.

To take each of the above memories and observations and reflections and philosophical statements and project to today's life style, one can see right away how our society has evolved into the situation I state above. For example: Religion has all but disappeared from the scene except in churches, and even there, corruption has become common and severe enough to cause divisions and the beginnings of thousands of "new" churches. It seems that when a person gets on the outs or even disagrees with the "preacher," they get themselves "ordained," without the benefit of attending a legitimate seminary, and start their own brand of religion and build a new "church" and accrues a new congregation which "believes" as they do. More time is spent in this arena than is spent in actually finding out what God really expects of them and how to live their lives in order to reach Heaven themselves. They assume they are the almighty masters and are so perfect themselves the start teaching everyone else to live the way they "believe." But another force is at work, too.

If the powers that be and those agnostic believers had their ways, the discussion of God and prayer would be "outlawed" even in churches because ... "It is being forced upon those who have the 'right' to not hear the prayer by another person. Ridiculous? Maybe! Maybe not! Actually, no one has a "right" to *not* hear a prayer to God. In fact, those very people, in my estimation and by God's teachings must not only hear those prayers, but they must be taught to believe in God and offer up their own prayers if they ever expect to enter Heaven themselves! Even if they do not believe in God, they must be taught about Him if at all possible. That was the instruction of Jesus to His disciples prior to His ascension.

Yes, I do remember! But, the new society wants not to remember, and since the current society contains many more affluent people than any previous society, the children of the better-off and politically powerful families are favored, and little or no punishment exists for their disrespect and crimes, just some psychological rhetoric and a hand slap and a spoiled and disrespectful person.

But after all that happened during the great depression, and all that has been caused by it, the questions remain: "Just 'WHAT' and 'WHO' should the master "psychologists" be "researching" and "studying?" Their main "proof," so called, is "...Studies show..." It could be that they should be on a desert island studying "each other." "...and just how far from accurate are their hypothesis pertaining to what the actual real people thought, did, and said while living out the depression years? (Some of their reasoning I've heard is truly ridiculous and far from reality, and the reasons people actually did those things and thought those things were so far from the psychologists phony "theories," it is pathetic.) "Just what is the effect on a society which advocates and practices 'absolute freedom,' as has been the new and incorrect interpretation of the First Amendment of our Constitution?' I ask.

The depression should have reminded us all of the high moral and social values we once had and the respect we once had for each other which have all gone down the tube. However, the influence of other societies from abroad since the "war" has infiltrated our own society and corrupted it with the notion of "absolute-freedom." So, now, we are what we are largely because of it. Can we ever return to the morals we once knew? I believe not...NOT without God being returned to the scene! And you know what? Our young people at this writing, have absolutely NO concept or intelligent vision of what the "good old days" were like nor how, in truth, morality governed the masses, and that immorality and crime involved itself with fewer, unlike the present-day society which is flooded with younger folks under forty who are "spoiled" into expecting the "good times" and "riches" of so called prosperity without having to actually earn these things over a long period of most of their lifetimes. Progress? Indeed not! Regress? Indeed yes!

However, we did have so many other experiences which were not only interesting and pleasant, but we learned how to survive and be team members in the community with little in the way of material things. We also learned to make the items we required in order to do specific things. For example, when we needed a certain tool that we didn't have, we had to make it. This resulted in becoming mechanics, carpenters, welders, blacksmiths, harness makers, and most anything else that was needed. So as children grew, they automatically learned those things as they were required. This happened automatically because the sons always worked alongside the fathers and the daughters worked alongside the mothers. (This has all but disappeared during recent "modern" times and affluent families who are taught to go "buy" everything, much to the detriment of the offspring of all families because all children at an early age are given the luxuries of life such as computers, automobiles, excessive spending money and such items that should be earned by the sweat of their own brows.) Some examples of this training are cited in the following paragraphs.

During the early thirties, the depression was well under way even though it really didn't hurt us on the homestead so badly. Actually, the most obvious problem we experienced was the lack of money. But we really did not absolutely require money, so to speak, as did the city dweller, in order to pay their rent and food and so forth. We paid no rent, we owned our land. We raised our food. We made our clothes. We, some of us, even made our vehicles and tractors and plows. The man of the place had been raised by his father to do the same, and his father before him. So it was just natural for us kids to work alongside Dad, since we were both boys. (Our sister, Jewel, arrived some fifteen years later, but was under the tutelage of our mother and worked alongside of her and learned to be a girl, a female, a mother, a home maker, and a wife.) So life in our part of the country was interesting and happy and produced self-sufficient individuals for the most part.

To begin the story, I need to mention that in the early thirties we had little money. We did have an old Ford car which had been set aside for lack of tires and gasoline and a battery to run it. So it sat by the corral fence for a few years rusting and being robbed of parts for other uses. Also the old truck was setting inside the corral next to another fence for the same reasons. In essence, all we used for transportation was a wagon and a team of horses. The wagon? Yes! Yes! You catch on fast! We built it!! From junk parts of several kinds of machines: Back wheels from an old discarded well drilling machine, front wheels from an old discarded iron-wheeled wagon, the wagon tongue and double tree and single trees and neck yoke were hewed from wood by us, the wagon bed built from used scrap lumber left over from the house, and the axle grease used to grease the wheels was NEW and purchased at the Claunch general store for ten cents for a one pound can of it and was stowed in the wagon for immediate use whenever a wheel began squealing . This wagon was used for about fifteen years for all things from hauling stove wood from the mountains seven miles away, to hauling water from a windmill three miles away, or a dirt tank (called a pond in the middlewest), some four miles away. We also cleaned it up and traveled the five and a half miles to Claunch to attend church services every Sunday. This continued until the economy improved so we could once again afford to purchase a car for the purpose. This was in 1935 when the U.S. Government paid all World War One veterans their "Bonus" benefits for "serving their country." Dad received his and used it to buy a 1929 Model A Ford Fordor sedan. I remember when he drove it home from Albuquerque where he had bought it from the Poe Motor Company. It looked just like new! I still remember the beautiful mohair upholstery, and I believe it was the most comfortable car I ever sat in, bar none.

We were still farming with horses and horse-drawn plows. A few other farmers who were a bit more affluent had managed somehow to buy tractors and pay for them at harvest time. But Dad, being the person he was, did not believe in going into debt like that, so he began building himself a tractor to farm with. He used the engine from the old truck and other parts from where ever he could find the parts he thought he needed for the job. He worked all winter on it. He also built the tractor-mounted plows for it. He made the necessary modifications to automobile and truck parts and shafts and gears. He became quite adept at machining and blacksmithing and designing. We boys worked alongside him and helped with running the drill press and forge and where ever we were needed when we weren't in school. Spring came, and the fields thawed. The tractor was put to work! Dad was a very happy person and was so proud of his "new tractor." However, time revealed that it was just too small to do the farming job that was required of it. So Dad had to go into debt for the then-huge amount of $200 to buy a used 1930 International Harvester Farmall "Regular" tractor. There was only one problem, however. It had NO implements with it! No lister, no planter, no cultivator, no harvester, no anything! So guess what! Yep, he had to build those implements. He did. He had to build them in his makeshift "blacksmith shop" Mom's very own kitchen.

The kitchen cook stove was the only place where he could build a fire out of the winter weather and in a place big enough to place the pieces of steel in and heat to a cherry red so he could forge and bend them into the required shapes needed to create those badly needed implements. I remember getting off the school bus in front of the house and hearing the "bang," "bang," bang," "ringgggg" from Dad's sledge emitting from inside the house as he formed those red-hot pieces of steel. Yes, he, of necessity that winter built those implements he needed to raise the crops of pinto beans, corn, soy beans, pumpkins, and turnips the following season. Yes, and they worked fine as he had planned them to. Dad was so proud. Those were the implements I learned to farm with, and I was so proud of them and Dad. We farmed with them several years up until the war started in 1941.

But that wasn't all! We had no truck! That first tractor had utilized its engine and transmission. We tried continuing to use the wagon and did for quite some time, but it could not be used to haul our crops to market in the nearest town, some 45 miles away. So guess what again!!! Yep!! We boys built one!! I mean us boys! Dad had no part of it. Actually, he didn't believe we could do it. It was built from parts from several kinds of machines. It was a very interesting truck, but worked great and lasted many years doing hard work, and it saved Dad a lot of money on hauling. It was a "duke's mixture" truck. The frame and wheels and axles were 1927 Chevrolet. The engine was mixed 1927 and 1928 Chevrolet parts, but Don and I redesigned them to work together. The radiator was retrieved from Uncle Jess's pasture and had been discarded from an old (1910) Cletrac bulldozer. The truck had no cab. The seat was a box we built from wood and cushioned with an old hooked rug Mom had made, used, and discarded. The steering wheel had no rim, but just the four metal spokes. The windshield was from a 1927 Ford coupe. There were no fenders which made it interesting driving in the heavy mud. The truck bed was built by Don and myself out of used lumber and made to look like a factory job by adding flared wings on the side boards.

By this time, Dad and we boys had managed to build a basic blacksmith shop next to the corral and the windmill where most of the farm machinery and other related items were kept some hundred yards from the house. This shop included a forge that Don and I designed and built from an old barrel that we cut in half and piped air into from a home-made blower we powered with an old Model A Ford transmission turned in reverse and furnished with a hand crank which we took turns turning. As I mentioned earlier, no electrical energy existed within 45 miles, so all power was supplied by whatever method we could dream up and build. Back to the truck.

This truck was used by us boys and by Dad for years. Yes, Dad finally saw that we did have the expertise to actually build the truck and developed some faith in us, and he actually liked the truck we built well enough to use it often in his work around the farm. I even drove it to do many jobs around the place including using it for a hay ride for a school celebration one night into the country side. Oh! I neglected to mention that it had no good lights on it. The headlights were there, but the generator had bad brushes in it which arced and would burn out the light bulbs immediately. So we just drove by the moonlight or starlight, whichever was the case. We never had an accident, nor was the truck ever licensed, nor did we ever have driver's licenses. (I never heard of licenses until I started to high school in Tularosa. Note: The only people in the area that had licenses were the ones who had to make trips to the city.) If someone else had to go to town, they would just "borrow" the license plates from whoever had some. Can't do that now!!

These were examples of some of the things people had to do routinely to survive. But we didn't look at it that way! We just went from day to day. We didn't look at it as "surviving". It was what we "did' in life. It wasn't given a thought. Whatever was needed we either had or didn't have. If we didn't have it and truly needed it, we improvised somehow.

A man was judged on his wisdom and his ability to improvise and for his ingenuity and inventiveness to do either with what he had at hand or could earn with honest work. This is something the modern world doesn't understand – **HARD WORK!** As we are all aware, modern people at the time of this writing demand huge salaries for *no* work, just let the machine or system do it for them.

Those were times that perhaps most likely shall never repeat themselves, but many memories linger and cause one to, for a brief moment in time, wonder whether people are more or, actually, less fortunate in these so-called modern times with endless amounts of money and credit [cards] and material things and spare time aplenty. Yes, in those days, one, of great necessity, spend most all of their time working. Yes, all average people had to work to eat, to have shelter, to have clothing, to pay cash for their things, in most cases. It is such a sobering feeling to envision one in this year of 2000 A.D. to be faced with the same requirements...**WORK...HARD WORK!** For little pay, and pay *cash* for everything!

Those were also times when our Christmas's were low key, but very happy and meaningful with regard to the true meaning of the season. Since money was an item we only talked about and didn't possess in any quantity beyond minimal farm expenses, the weeks prior to Christmas day were spent making by hand our gifts which we intended for the family members. Mom usually made items of clothing on her sewing machine for each of us. Mittens were the usual thing for us boys, perhaps a "new" shirt made-over from one of Dad's. Dad usually made an item of wood such as a toy wagon or something on that order, but kept it well hidden from our view until Christmas morning. One instance comes to mind, in particular.

There seemed an almost eerie atmosphere about the house for several weeks during the autumn of 1932. I did not, at the time, realize that my parents weren't working during the day while us kids were in school which left the entire time unto themselves, as I look back. However, I recall that from the time we got off the school bus in the afternoon, around five o'clock, the folks were a little "extra" busy about the business of getting supper and cleaning up the house. I noticed the house work being done in the afternoon instead of the morning, but

I didn't pay any attention to it, for some reason. I also recall the folks being a little extra friendly toward each other, too. This continued until Christmas morning. One thing that did get my attention was that I detected this strong odor of fresh paint, but for the life of me I couldn't find any new paint. Nowhere! Of course, all I received from the folks when I inquired was some excuse of something that was painted that got scratched or something.

M E E E E R R R R Y C H R I S S S S T M A S!!!! I awakened immediately! I actually had planned to stay awake that night and catch Dad up to his Santa tricks, but he out foxed me, for he knew I would fall asleep eventually.

Dad and Mom were up already, and had employed this loud and well-articulated exclamatory burst of vocal energy to separate two sleeping young lads from their dreams and get them involved in the holiday's festivities. I must say, "It worked!" . The candles were burning brightly on the Christmas tree. We used real candles in holders on the pinyon pine Christmas tree which we had just a few weeks before decorated with homemade construction paper chains of red and green and with popcorn garlands which we had strung on a string. Also there was a large homemade star at the apex and colored glass balls hanging all around in a sea of long pure lead icicles. How beautiful!

No sooner had Dad yelled the greeting of the season, than Don and I were into our pants (we couldn't afford pajamas or night clothes, we just slept naked), as we raced to the tree pulling up our trousers as we ran to see what had our names written on homemade paper tags attached. NOW, it all made perfect sense! That big green wagon with red wheels, all made of wood. Yes! Both our names were on that tag! It was the most beautiful coaster wagon I had ever seen in my life. Dad was always so talented with the old handed-down wood working tools and carpentry. Now, we knew what the strange eeriness was all about that had been hanging over the Easley home for several weeks. They had been making the wagon! And the paint? Yep! The wagon! But I was curious! Where had they hidden it? Mom looked at Dad, Dad said, "Up in the ceiling." (He always referred to the attic as the "ceiling.")

And so were the Christmases at our house in those days. Most all toys and other presents were home-made using our hands and all the love we could muster.

There were homemade cookies from Mom's talents, and there were German cookies and nuts sent by Grandma and Grandpa Malleis and there was baked chicken and dressing and all the trimmings, and there was story-telling and singing and Bible readings and prayer both before the meal and after. God had blessed us all for another year and for another season.

No, we didn't know we were poor. But we did know who we were and where we were and we loved each other, and we were content and never even dreamed of wanting to be elsewhere doing other things with someone else. We also were informed. We also heard through several channels of information there were a lot of cities in trouble, a lot of hungry people in bread lines (however, we had no idea of what a bread line even was, having never experienced one.). We saw the pictures in magazines and papers and heard people speak on the radio of gangsters, of homeless people living on streets, of armies fighting each other around the world, of people dying from many causes, and felt truly sorry for them and their situations. We had prayer at home, in school, and at church on Sunday for these people, and we asked God to help them, and we thanked Him for being so good to US, because we had the things they didn't. We had food and a good bed, even though most were home-made from straw or cotton. But, at least, we had shelter which cost nothing, it was ours! Also, we had love in our families. We were grateful, very grateful, indeed! But most of all, we respected our elders, most especially OUR PARENTS! Also, we were taught in church, at school and at home that the father was the head of the family and responsible for the family's upbringing, religious training, and debts. We were also taught that the mother was second in command in the family and deserved her due respect as such. We were also taught that children had to spend their minor years learning and training with their parents at the helm so they, the children, might be duly qualified to take on the adult responsibilities and to eventually deserve the respect of an adult and parent. Children having "equal rights" of the parents? NO! Not until they reached the age of majority. Even then, respect for their parents and for their elders was to continue forever!

These are my personal reflections and my personal experiences and some of the details of my upbringing which are "typical" of those of most country folks back then. One may choose to disagree with them, but having lived through those times personally, I state what I truly was taught, saw, lived, and believed and do believe! If there are those who dare to disagree with what I say here, my comment to them is this:

One would be well advised to rethink their position and life experiences and to realize they need to have been there in my shoes themselves, personally, and to have experienced the same situations in order to speak wisely and truthfully about them. But in the event those persons have never experienced what I herein describe, then, my learned suggestion to them is this: Since you lack the actual experiences and the wisdom taught by each experience, I suggest you render your negative mouths inoperative and exert great effort toward the learning process from each of our situations during those difficult times, and apply that knowledge to your own life's story.

I need to mention, before going any farther, that, in spite of the hardships, there were so many experiences that offset the negative ones by far. There were humorous experiences, entertaining experiences, and just plain stupid ones, too. The following story I will leave up to the reader to classify into whatever category they wish, but I prefer to place it into the "interesting" category myself.

Our close friend John Montgomery and his brother Roy lived about seven miles to the west of our place where they owned a small cattle ranch on adjoining homesteads which they had combined into one ranching operation. They had built an underground "dugout" type house which had the roof constructed to be about a foot above the ground level with small windows located in those very short walls. They also had built a fireplace into the wall with the chimney extending well above the roof to prevent downdrafts. Inside, it was well furnished, considering they were both bachelors, in very rustic home-made western ranch furniture of rawhide with the red and white hair of the Hereford outward for appearance and comfort. The fireplace was of native limestone rocks laid as bricks with a wooden mantle of pine timber about six feet long across the top.

John was the elected republican state representative with his office in Santa Fe, the state capital of New Mexico. Roy stayed around the place and took care of the livestock and fields. However, they had a very unusual avocation in common, that of snake hunting. Yes Sir! Diamond Back Rattlesnakes! Their land holdings were just at the eastern edge of the mountainous foothills to the west which were covered with Utah Juniper and Pinyon Pine, limestone caves, AND Diamond Backs. Their snare was made of a long green juniper branch the size of a man's thumb with a leather boot strap tied to the other end. The leather strap had a slip loop made into its end which could be lowered over the snake's head as it lay coiled at a distance. A **QUICK JERK** ... and all hell would break loose! Those diamond backs were one wild, mad, and strong, and vicious breed, and always anxious to start a fight! In addition, they were a large snake and plenty strong, strong enough in fact that two men were usually required to subdue one of these ferocious beasts. Certainly **NO** hobby for the city boy.

But the clincher to this story is that the fellows preferred to enter these caves with a light and the snake stick and locate a big rattle snake and capture it alive, drag it out of the cave and show it off to the neighbors and friends by driving about the countryside with it in a gunny sack in the back of their Plymouth pickup before skinning it. It must be explained at this point that rattle snakes are attracted to a light and will go toward it and attack it. So we non-snake-hunting folks always considered it very unwise, to say the least, if not downright stupid to use a light to snake hunt inside a cave, or anywhere else, for that matter. In fact, we considered it very unwise just to enter a cave in rattlesnake country, if not just plain stupid!

But be all that as it may, Ed and I had reason to visit John and Roy one day and drove over to their ranch. After the usual "Hi, how are ya? Come on in, I want to show ya something." There above the mantle next the ceiling was hung the skin of his latest trophy, a skin that extended the length of the mantle with the head end of the snake skin hanging down about eighteen inches. The rattle-end of the skin hanging down on the opposite end of the mantle was about another eighteen inches. The total length of that skin would have measured about nine feet if stretched out straight. The skin was flattened out against the wall and measured well over eighteen inches in width. To put this snake in perspective for those unfamiliar with rattle snakes, that snake would have looked like a 6-inch stove pipe nine feet long with rattles as wide as a man's hand and a head much wider.

This dangerous serpent was taken on a boot strap by the Montgomery boys from a limestone cave on their ranch one day in 1941, the best I remember. In addition to being idiots, I contend they are to be called heroes just for being able to outrun that snake out of the cave!

To the north of the northwest corner of our homestead place, about fifty feet from our north fence, was located a small limestone cave opening. This opening measured about ten or so feet in length and about two or three feet wide and tapered in depth to a small crack between two rocks which probably measured about a foot in width and tapered to nothing at each end. It was too small for a person to enter without some excavation effort. This cave entrance was of little interest to most, especially during the winter months. But during early spring, it was a much different story.

Strangers to the area would have considered it just a strange opening in the gently sloping hillside, but the natives always steered clear of this place, and with very good reason. They knew from experience to keep their distance because this little cave was much larger just under the surface and was the historical home of hundreds of thousands of prairie rattlers. These rattle snakes were smaller than the diamond back rattlers in the foothills, but were just as poisonous although they were only about two to four feet in length. Their temperament was most terrible and they were *always* looking to pick a fight. They were always ready and quite able to fight almost anything, and the sound of their rattle would most always cause one to require dry trousers upon a surprise encounter.

But back to the cave. Each spring, the warmth of the earth's surface near the cave opening signaled the huge masses of rattlers, young and old alike, to emerge from the cave's depths and sun in huge entwined matted masses of the snakes which positioned themselves around the perimeter of the cave for a distance of a few dozen feet. The masses of serpents would gradually disassemble from their entanglement and disburse over a period of about a month or so and expand their range until during mid-summer they were to be found at distances up to two or three miles or more from the cave entrance.

Our neighbor to the northeast, Finis Jones, usually kept close tabs on these creatures and when they would first start appearing in the spring, he would take his wagon and team and lunch and plenty of 410 shotgun ammunition and park his wagon about twenty or so feet from the cave entrance. His team, he unhooked and tied up to our fence some hundred or so yards away. He spent all day, day in and day out for about a month, shooting rattle snakes from the safety of his perch on that wagon as they came out of the cave. As a usual day's efforts he claimed a normal kill of about two to three hundred snakes. But even after he ceased efforts and redirected his efforts to his farm work, there were still a huge number of snakes that migrated to the surrounding farms. So we had to constantly be on guard for the critters and we never left the house without our snake sticks.

Finis' wife, Ala, (the first A was pronounces as a *long A)* the school teacher, gathered the necessary information from Finis and would write and submit a regular article reporting Finis' activities as the states most well-known snake hunter and killer. This article was published monthly in the *New Mexico* magazine for many years running.

CHAPTER 5

* * *

PIONEER COUNTRY SCHOOL OUT WEST ...... SECOND TO NONE!!

When homesteading was in its infancy in central New Mexico, a very interesting situation presented itself to the homesteaders which urban dwellers across early America had never experienced, at least to any appreciable degree. They had children, but there were no schools. The families whom had made the move out west did, most of them, have young children which were of school age or who would be soon. However, those families were disbursed over several hundreds of square miles, and as iterated previously, lived no closer than one mile apart. This is because their land sections were a mile square. So each family lived on the average of a mile from their neighbor. So, also, if each family had one child of school age, it would require twenty square miles to supply twenty children to a small school. However, in reality, things were a bit different from that hypothetical example.

The truth was that each family did not live a mile apart because not every section of land was claimed by homestead. Some families homesteaded some ten miles apart, some, six, some three, some twenty, and some one mile apart. So in truth, the families in our community were scattered over an area measuring some twenty four miles long by sixteen miles wide, some 384 square miles. This was the area concerned with the small locale if immediate interest of forming a school district comprising the homesteaders in our upland-valley". Dad was very involved in getting things rolling for a school, a church, and a post office in this community. He spent many hours traveling to the county seat town of Socorro about 75 miles to the west in the Rio Grande Valley. Others joined in the effort and, by 1928, they had succeeded in getting the post office and school approved. First was a post office. It was named *Fairview"*. Later, Mr. Charles Claunch bought land a few miles to the northwest to enlarge his sheep ranch, and actually joined the fight to get politicians to agree to build a school in *Fairview*. With all this new assistance from Mr. Claunch, and this added influence in the county seat pertaining to local efforts, the people of the community decided to change the name of the new post office to the **Claunch** Post Office. This was the beginning of the village of Claunch, New Mexico. The "village" itself amounted to just one frame building which was constructed by Mr. Petross and his wife, new immigrants from Texas, who had not yet homesteaded but elected to apply for the Postmaster's job and install the post office in this building, their home. A year or so later they added a general store addition to the building and did homestead on the section of land as their own which Mr. Petross did farm.

Photo Showing Street Scene as it Appears Today.

Another sheep rancher consented to let the new school use a hundred-year-old, unoccupied adobe sheep herder's house for its classes until a school building as such could be built. This adobe house was perhaps ten feet wide inside by about sixteen feet long. It had a rusty red corrugated iron roof with no ceiling. It had one single glass window on the south end and one on the north end. The home-made door was situated midway on the ease wall with no step. An outhouse (2-holer) was constructed about fifty feet to the south of the building for use by the school kids and teacher. Our neighbor, Ala Jones, had applied for the teaching job and was hired. She and her husband, Finis, lived on a section of land which joined ours on the northeast corner. I mention this because she had to drive past our house on the way to teach at the little adobe school in Claunch. Claunch was situated one mile west and four miles south of our section (refer to the map presented in a previous chapter). So my first two years were spend in the little adobe one-room school on the little hill a quarter mile northeast of the post office. What memories!! What experiences for a five-year-old boy!! Before I continue, I just must tell you two of the experiences.

The 2-holer outhouse just mentioned was the scene of many interesting events, and I find it compelling to describe just one of them...involving *me*!

I plainly recall one day Mrs. Jones was teaching us all the things we needed to know about "money;" identification and values of various coins, bills and the like. It's important here to note that I, normally, had to take immediate action when I got the urge to urinate, otherwise, disaster! So, guess what? During this class session, I had to go. Right in the middle of class! I had to go really bad! I held up my two small fingers in a "vee" (which meant I had to go to the toilet). Mrs. Jones nodded her head and I wasted no time arriving at the outhouse. I swung open the door and BEHOLD!! Gladys, my 5-year-old classmate, was standing there in front of the other hole with her bloomers down crying, crying uncontrollably. Well, I could see her problem right away! She had a bad case of diarrhea. She had missed the hole. The entire seat was a mess! Not only did I feel sorry for her, but I really had to GO, but first, I had to clean the seat! So I reached in my jacket pocket and pulled out my brand-new mittens that Mom had just bought me for the winter weather. I proceeded to clean up the seat with them. One got "dirty" and I dropped it into the hole in front of me. I used the other mitten to finish "cleaning up", but, then, something told me that I had to keep it. It was new, and I didn't want Mom to spank me for "losing" it. So I stuck it back into my jacket pocket and decided I had to have the other one too. So I reached into the hole and retrieved the first one and put it into the same pocket with the other one. I figured I was now clear of any wrath from Mom. Then, on the borderline of a *real* catastrophe, I finally got to do my thing. I returned to the school house so relieved that I forgot to notice the situation at the next hole. But a while later Gladys returned to the classroom…still crying. Mrs. Jones had little to say on the trip home after school was out, but Mom had a lot to say after Mrs. Jones dropped me off at my home, not to mention the thorough bath I had to take. I was also instructed on how I was *never* to clean up someone else's "mess".

This year, 1929, was memorable in more than one way. Of course, most every one of my age remembers that the stock market and banks started failing during this year, and so many other stories began, also. There were those who lost their fortunes, those who lost their homes, those who were born, and those who died. But for me, it was my first year in school. It was the year I started school, age five. In the pioneer west where we lived, one started school at age five and began in the first grade. Oh, there was an introductory few weeks called "Primer" where the teacher taught us kids to play and study together without each doing our own thing. Our teacher taught us as a conductor conducts his orchestra…in concert. Very interesting, because in today's schools each child is pressured to be "independent" of everyone else, even of his or her parents, in the learning arena.

In those days which some of the "modern" people refer to as "the old days," the teacher included every child, boys and girls alike, in everything she did. (I use the feminine gender here because most teachers were female, at least in the lower grades.) She taught them to do the activity at hand *together* as a "team" and have respect for each other, and be in a *happy mode*. She began out of doors with games. We all became *acquainted* with each other, first, under the guidance of the ever-observant eye of the teacher. We played friendly games together under her detailed supervision. Games such as "Ring around the Rosie" and "London Bridge is Falling Down" and "Drop the Handkerchief" were played during recess times and after we had eaten our lunches from our "dinner buckets". (Dinner buckets were those empty syrup and jelly half-gallon buckets with bails and lids which were saved by our parents to be used to pack our lunches in for school. Our lunches usually were quite alike and very consistent from day-to-day: A couple of biscuit sandwiches made with either home-made sausage, or fried eggs, or venison, or peanut butter. If apples were available from a peddler, we had an apple in our bucket. We, of course, were very familiar with peanut butter sandwiches, but only when we made a good crop were we fortunate enough to buy such a luxury as a gallon bucket of peanut butter which sold for a rather high cost of about sixty cents, maybe even more at times. But when we did manage to procure this revered "staple," we thought we were in Heaven and exercised great sagacity in its usage.)

Other games such as Marbles, "Mumble Peg" (with either a fully-open or a half folded pocket knife), "Top" spinning, "Over the River," and others were also played by all us kids. Again, we were all included and supervised. We not only learned the game, but how to play it as a team effort, each doing his or her part well and unselfishly. As I look back, I see that the ground work was laid back then when I was both young enough to learn discipline, and before what I call **mind-set** had begun. (This usually starts in small degrees after the sixth birthday. It is my experience and observation that most of the things a person learns is learned between birth and age six.) Anyway, by mid-winter, we were into the main subjects at hand. I remember these too included a very important teaching technique not used today except by the Montessori schools. The combined-subject technique to achieve total understanding and skills in each of the subjects were treated simultaneously. In this method of teaching, the children were guided in teaching themselves the subjects with special emphasis on training all of their senses in each of the particular subjects as they were learned. This is a very great method of teaching even very difficult subjects such as the more advanced principles of number relationships to first graders in a manner such that the child totally understands every facet of the numerical manipulation they have performed. This included the relationships between addition and multiplication and how multiplication is just an extended form of addition. The same was true for subtraction and division of numbers; division being another form of subtraction. Then how multiplying a number times itself had a distinct and unique way of adding themselves together as many times as the number itself. Wow! What a fun "game" this became. So squaring numbers and extracting "roots" were all demonstrated with physical items, and the kids actually worked with familiar items such as grains of corn or beans and the like to imitate and become familiar with what the teacher had just demonstrated. Much time and care was allowed so the student might thoroughly understand the principals involved. The teacher was constantly on her feet going from one child to the other, over and over, and over again, ensuring individual relationships with the varying capabilities of the many children. It has to be remembered that the teacher taught all eight grades simultaneously in one room. No child left the class without a good understanding of number relationships. (This certainly is not the case in schools today where my children and others I know have attended.) This method I have also witnessed in the beginning classes at the elementary school department at Notre Dame University near San Francisco, California.

My first teacher, Mrs. Jones, as I mentioned earlier, did not possess a college degree of any kind. However, she was an expert at teaching using this method but not referred to as the Montessori Method until years later. It was a common-sense method of teaching a subject of any type, and as I remember, she taught the alphabet (upper and lower case), penmanship, lettering, numbers and counting *ad infinitum, and reading phonetically,* all at the same time...together! As she taught the letter "A" she would show us all the ways to write it, pronounce it, sound it out, and use it, and count the times we used it in a word, in a sentence, and to feel a wooden model of it all in the same operation, not to mention its position as a note on the pump-organ keyboard, then hear and remember its pitch sound. What a wonderful teacher she was. We were taught how to "write" it and "print" it. This was done with each letter and number. Examples were "real words," not stupid nonsensical words. We were taught to behave and respect all others, especially God, and older persons, if only one day older. We also started every day by saluting the flag of the United States, and the Pledge of Allegiance.

Then she led us in prayer just as was done on Sunday when we went to church. By the way, we were taught the differences between "rights and "privileges." (As an aside, it is MY belief tried and true that we actually have NO so-called "rights," but privileges instead. God grants us no rights. The "Bill of Rights," so called, is actually a misnomer. It should have been called "*The Bill of Privileges.*")

I mentioned all this because it has been very important in my subsequent life. Mrs. Jones may not have had all the "prestigious" education of a modern-day teacher (or "educator" as they like to be called), but her level of achievement as a teacher and molder of human lives was extremely high and cannot be ignored nor can it be easily equaled or exceeded by modern educators using their newly acquired psychology and unionized methods of teaching "confusion" in the class rooms. I stand as an example of her capability. I am a product of that little one-room adobe classroom and have lived a very professional and successful life in the professional arena of science and research and development engineering for both industry and the armed forces. When I entered Colorado State University some fourteen years subsequent to my graduation from Claunch High School, I passed all entrance tests with honors and did not require any make-up classes, but was asked, instead, to assist the professor in teaching the laboratory section of his engineering drafting class as a freshman. The knowledge required was acquired at Claunch and from my subsequent experiences based upon my schooling and abilities learned in that one room school by a non-"certified" teacher. So, also, education and degrees are just what one makes out of them; a lot? Or nothing! So many degrees are just framed and become a part of someone's wall decor and a "requirement" for employment. Some are genuine. Some are unearned.

No, hardly anyone ever heard of Claunch. But, I am proud to have had that experience, and I am proud to say that as a result of what I was taught there, I have come to leave my mark in this world. I can say truly that I, unbeknown to some but known to many, have contributed greatly to my Church and God's teachings through my participation and to my country through my contributions to the United States Naval Research Laboratories and to the field of scientific discovery and development at all levels through Doctoral.

Subsequent teachers varied in their backgrounds as do most other people and things differ in their characteristics. Mrs. Kennedy, for example, taught grades two through eight in one room. This classroom was in the first school building that had been built in 1930 as a result of Dad's efforts at the county seat lobbying for a school. Of course, others must be given credit, too, for it required efforts by several men to get the approvals required.

The building had only one room, windows on the sides, and a single door on the front facing the road to the east. As I mentioned earlier, all roads were just two tracks worn through the prairie grass which had been made by wagons and a few Ford cars of the twenties circa. Few fences had been constructed near the school as yet, so the school sat out in the prairie alone, so to speak. The children attending were transported for the most part by their parents somehow, and a few walked. No school busses existed as yet and didn't for another year. Mrs. Kennedy was a tall plump lady, single, and quite loving toward her students. I don't remember much about her as an educator, but I do remember we all liked her a lot. But there is one incident that I do remember that involved her.

Two of the older boys had arrived at school quite early that particular morning. They didn't live very far away, about two miles, and had come across a large bull snake on their way to school. Well, being the boys that they were, and at the age of mischievousness, they managed to capture that large snake, about four feet long, and bring it to school. Mrs. Kennedy had not arrived yet, so the boys opened her center desk drawer and placed the snake into the drawer and closed it.

The desk was situated at the far end of the room as one entered the front door. The children's desks all faced her desk. Everyone waited for her arrival, some wanted to tell her of her upcoming plight but too frightened to do so, and others too frightened to open their mouth for fear of retaliation by the boys. So we waited. Mrs. Kennedy finally entered the door and stood transfixed having stopped by the sight of all the kids already inside. Generally, she had to ring the bell to call them all in. But on this morning, she was totally surprised and puzzled to find them in their seats already.

She proceeded on up the isle to her desk and laid her things on it, removed her coat and hung it on the rack, stopped and looked at the kids for a moment and sat down on her wooden swivel chair. The kids began to snicker and giggle as she continued with her morning preparations. I don't remember all that transpired, it has been such a long time ago, but I do remember that she finally pushed her chair back a bit, then she pulled open the drawer, "eeeeeeeEEEEEEEEKKKKKKKKKK!!!!!!!," she screamed! She had spotted the snake, and it had spotted her! Out it came! It shot past her in a terrific effort to remove itself from the situation as fast as it possibly could. It jumped from the desk drawer to the floor at her feet, she jumped up onto the desk, the snake shot to one side of the room then to the other, slithered down the aisle, under desks, between kids' feet, kids screamed, the teacher screamed, and, finally, the snake found the open door and headed for the great expanse of the prairie land of New Mexico and hasn't been seen since. As I look back from time to time, I have, on occasion, contemplated the actual amount of laundry that was required immediately thereafter.

Such memories! Yes! I wonder whether city kids ever have such interesting and memorable milestones to chuckle about ?

But, there were many experiences which helped build and alter one's character.

CHAPTER 6

★ ★ ★

FROM LUXURIOUS COMFORT TO "BLOOD-SWEAT-AND-TEARS"

It needs to be said at this point that homesteading in the west during those times was anything but easy. In fact, when we pioneers migrated westward, not only did a lot of thought and planning take place for most who made the move. But, also, sacrifices so great that the city dweller can only guess or, at most, attempt to imagine were made and experienced by those brave enough and strong enough to dare to make such a drastic change in their lives . Those sacrifices were, for the most part, much greater than those dramatized in present day movies and other dramatizations, or taught in schools; history books contain only what certain people and organizations want them to contain. Fact is, most hearts were broken, many lives affected in so many ways, and human bodies were maimed by disease, accident, sunstroke, snakebite, marauders, starvation, and disappointment. Not mentioned thus far, is the fact that nearly all those families left loved ones behind thousands of miles away never to hear from or see them again.

Also, the agonies of existing without the luxuries and comforts of the lifelong homes they had left behind in order to attain the dreams that lay ahead were an inescapable part of nature's plan. Those destinations, for most, were never to be as golden and easy to realize as they were led to believe. Such was the case with my own parents, especially with Mom.

As explained earlier, Mom was the daughter of the Malleis clan which had immigrated from Prussia during the middle nineteenth century. They were always a very progressive and intelligent clan which usually strived to maintain a good lifestyle no matter what type of endeavor they would happen to follow for a livelihood. As a result, when they settled in central Kansas they built comfortable homes and accrued the niceties of life they each desired, and they lived in above average comfort.

Mom had a wonderful childhood. She was the only living daughter, her older sister, Etna, had died at the age of two months and was buried in the Moundridge Cemetery. Mom was not spoiled because Grandpa and Grandma Malleis absolutely didn't believe in that sort of thing, and did provide a very comfortable life for Mom and Carl, her older brother. They gave Mom a good education, piano lessons, and nurses training to boot. She was an attractive lady and always dressed well and made many lifelong friends. She also had many relatives living in the surrounding area. Some owned wheat farms, some owned stores, one was a postmaster, and others were attorneys or other tradesmen. So Mom was anything but a country girl just waiting to move to the dry, cactus covered, snake-ridden, dusty prairie of the west. Nor was she prepared either physically or mentally to be a homesteader's wife and a mother of his children which she would have to help nurture and raise and educate in the throes of poverty and hardship which would be quite foreign to her upbringing and training. But Mom being the gentile and true lady that she was dedicated herself to Dad and to her wedding vows, and to God, her most loved Heavenly Father. So with all this, she and Dad headed westward to a new life in a new place to them much distant from everything that made them secure in their minds and hearts. "Heavenly Father, be with us," she prayed almost daily thereafter.

The actual move to the homestead was actually rather pleasant and, as Mom described it, "a kind of vacation trip." The countryside they traveled through was new to them, and the people they met were friendly and some became friends with whom they corresponded for several years to come. The first few months of setting up their new "home" in a borrowed vacant ranch house was a challenge and interesting, I remember Mom saying. However, the pleasures of it all soon eroded and life became such a challenge that Mom tearfully began remembering the comforts she had left behind in Newton.

Her new "yard" consisted of the miles of prairie visible from her door in all directions without the sight of any nearby neighbor's house whatsoever. It consisted of the thousands of prairie rattlesnakes which emerged from their dens each spring just to migrate for miles among the prairie grasses and take up residence under any nearby object that offered them shade. Mom didn't know how to kill one of them, but it was often required of her anyway as a matter of self-defense and to protect her firstborn, me, from certain death as I played in that "yard."

It consisted, also, of the blowing dust which penetrated every crack and crevice in that old house which made the pleasure of keeping house a real drudgery and often required a shovel instead of a broom. Her yard also comprised all those thousands of acres of surrounding grass and cactus covered land which served not only as beautiful scenery, but as her toilet which she had to learn to squat upon, and to use the nearest weeds, rocks, sticks, or whatever in remembrance of that ever-so-soft tissue of her past.

Our Homestead Home, 1930.

Her new "home" was that haven of rest for the weary where 6-inch centipedes thrived and shared the space under boards, behind the packing paper used to chink cracks around doors, windows, and between the boards of the floor. Her new "home" also was a place where her cooking utensils and every bucket possessed by the family had a necessary purpose under the dozens of leaks during the several rainstorms of summer. Her new "home" was a haven, a blessed haven for the family to sit together, eat together pray together and hold worship services together on the Holy days of Obligation. God lived in that "home," right along with the rest of us, Mom said. She said He gave us the strength to learn and to persevere.

With the passing of time and the changes of the seasons, Dad and Grandpa Jim finished the homestead house to a point that they could move us into our "new" home on our own place! What a glorious occasion Mom told us in later years. The folks busied themselves doing the necessary jobs to finish up small tasks of hanging the windows and doors and installing the stoves. Dad's other jobs that required a huge amount of his time and sweat were the building of corral fences and pasture fences to keep the cows and horses out of the fields (still to be broken from the sod), and to keep the animals on our own property. Mom found herself digging post holes while Dad chopped and hauled cedar fence posts on the wagon from the forest some three or four miles away. They would both, then, set the posts in the holes and tamp the dirt back around them in order to make them solid and immoveable. Barbed wire was then rolled out alongside the posts for an entire mile at a time, and stretched and stapled to the posts a quarter mile at a time because the barbed wire came on quarter-mile spools. This was terrifically hard work, even for Dad. But Moms agony was so much more strenuous and painful simply because she was a very petite woman doing a big man's work. She was never again to have those nice filed fingernails that she knew during the days of her city life, but the calloused and bleeding hands of a homesteader's wife instead.

Mom's hands, as I have already mentioned, were calloused. So badly calloused were they that care had to be taken as she put on her stockings not to snag the threads on her hands.

Large cracks would appear on her hands as they did on all our hands during the cold and dry winter months. This chapping was a terrible thing to experience because it would never heal but bleed constantly. We had to keep our hands wrapped and treated with hog fat to keep them soft during those months. It was very heartbreaking to witness Mom writing to Grandpa Malleis in Newton while trying as she did to endure the pain from those chapped and calloused hands.

But Mom was a trooper. She was loyal. She was a very hard worker and did Dad's kind of work without a whimper that was to be heard by anyone, that is, by anyone except a couple of concerned small sons, myself and Don, who would hide and cuddle together and cry for her. She was a loving Mom, a dedicated Mom a slave; she weighed 92 pounds.

Mom, being of more-or-less elite upbringing, still felt the need to occasionally put on her nicer dresses, which she had brought with her from Newton. A journey by wagon to Grandpa Jim's house was not a regularly-scheduled thing, nor was it a legitimate reason to "dress up," but it did give her an excuse to wear those clothes which had hung in the make-shift closet all those years. But, it was an outing of sorts and she seemed to enjoy the occasion. Then when Sunday came, it was a much different situation there on the homestead.

Since there was no real church within forty five miles, Mom and Dad felt that on Sunday, a Holy Day, the Church services were to be held at home with Dad reading from the Holy Bible first, then Mom. They would sing from an old hymnal, and we all worshiped our God from our own "Tabernacle." Mom got to wear her nice dress and Dad his old-but-clean suit. Oh, yes! Don and I were introduced to little shirts and ties that Mom made for us from some of their old cast off garments. Mom put her grandmother's beautiful hand crocheted lace table cloth over the oil cloth on our home-made kitchen table, got down her nice Haviland china, and we were proud to be God's children, like the Bible Dad read to us said we were.

The springs turned to summers, the autumns turned to winters, then spring again. Years passed. We boys never kept count, but I am sure Mom and Dad counted the long and miserable seasons of hard work that collectively built that new homestead into whatever sort of a farm it was, but still with only water which had to be hauled by wagon from the neighboring ranches some miles distant. Mom put in her share of driving that team hitched to that rough-riding, steel-wheeled wagon over that cow-trail road, loading water from the dirt tank (called a pond in the east), then later, from a knee tub metal tank, and home again. On arrival back home it had to be unloaded into barrels on the ground by siphoning it through a length of that garden hose which had been brought from Newton so many years previous. As we boys grew and matured and had enough strength, we inherited the water-hauling job, and poor Mom finally got her long deserved rest from it.

Dad also was a trouper and worked at his chores and field work and the making of farm implements as required. He also did not possess the least bit of obesity, for he could only boast about 160 pounds soaking wet! For a rather tall person, his overalls hung on him like a gunny sack, and his bewhiskered face didn't resemble that of the once-proud professional barber. Life was unkind and the days were long, and the sun tanned his once fair skin to a near leather-like complexion. Also, the dust and the ragweed pollen had no mercy on his hay fever, and the cold winter blizzards made asthma almost unbearable, and, for sure, we occasionally didn't expect him to pull through a few of those cold spells. Ultimately, and through necessity, this meant only one thing: We boys would have to take over all those jobs and chores that had been Dad's responsibilities for so long.

I was just entering into the second year of my second decade of life, and Don was just finishing his first decade when we together, with Mom's guidance and Dad's as best he could, assumed those responsibilities as best we two young half-scared boys could. Of course, we had been working as Dad's "helpers" for a few years, and that was a good thing. It gave us just that bit of self-confidence to know the work we were facing could actually be done, for we had either done it, or had seen Mom and Dad doing it. So we began our jobs with more than average zeal even though with a bit of uncertainty. For example, how deep were we suppose to plow in the fall to prepare the ground for winter, to "hold" the ground from blowing away, yet catching the neighbor's soil as it blew across our fields? Also, just how many inches between the bean seeds when we planted them? Which planter plate were we suppose to use to give that proper spacing of the beans? How was the proper adjustment of the "Go-Devil" knives and discs in order to cut all the weeds and yet not to cover up completely the young plants, but allow the dirt to be filled in around the plants to just under those two first leaves? So much to know and to learn. But learn we did. We boys were to be forever indebted to our dear Grandpa Jim, also, for his ever-so-wise assistance and guidance.

CHAPTER 7
* * *

A NEW ERA
A NEW SCHOOL DISTRICT
WHITE LAKE

By 1931, most land that had been made available for homesteading had been filed upon. Those who wished to live on their deeded section continued to do so and had either built or started construction of a home and barns and other improvements they had planned and could afford. Others chose to leave, for one reason or another, after the completion of their homesteading requirements. However, the usual reason they had was that the existence was too difficult and greener pastures existed elsewhere they thought. So those who chose to leave, sold their holdings to those who chose to stay. As a result, the sizes and shapes of the remaining holdings changed and resulted in a totally different gerrymandered community. This was interesting because gerrymandering usually refers to the "unfair manipulation of boundaries to favor one political group over another." This is exactly what happened although it was not planned per se'. The men who had the money to buy the others out did, in fact, have the money in hand. They had amassed the cash various ways, but, as applicable to the one who was principal in most land acquisitions thereabouts, the source was mostly from bootlegging moonshine. This was interesting in another way, too. This was that he had more political clout in the county seat than any other local man.

This left him the owner of the largest holdings of land, the largest farmer, the largest political lobbyist, and the largest money lender locally. One might say he was in control of the community without saying a word to anyone about anything. It just evolved into this situation. But another word must be said about him. He was, beyond a doubt, the kindest and friendliest and most generous man in the community. No person needed to go without help with Fred Shumate so willing and able.

With this changing of various political boundaries, there arose a need for a new school to the northwest of Claunch. This was due to several families being left in that quadrant of the county and isolated from the Claunch school by many miles which were the cause of the resulting large land holdings in that direction. So Dad got busy again and began lobbying for the new school. He knew that the original U.S.G.S. (U.S. Geological Survey) land survey during the late 1800s provided one "school section" in each township; a township being a square of 36 sections which measured six miles on each of the four sides. So Dad identified the school section in the "White Lake" area and proposed that a new school to be built on it.

The name **White Lake** was taken from the name of the natural lake situated in the section of land cornering the school section on the northeast. Almost the entire northern half of the section was relatively of lower elevation and formed a natural sump where water collected from the rains and usually formed a quite large lake of perhaps a hundred or more acres. When the sun dried up the water during dry seasons, the ground was left "white" from the saline encrustation left behind on the surface. Therefore, the name.

The proposal was approved and the school was, in fact, built. So in September, 1931, Don, my younger brother, and I made up part of the first student body there, I in the third grade and Don, my brother, beginning his first school year at the new *White Lake School* . This was a "big" school house to me. It boasted two rooms! It even had two front doors, one into each room, and a porch across the front without railings. No other building existed within three quarters of a mile, and that one was Mr. Gaines' house. Mr. Gaines was the brother-in-law to Uncle Jess, and they lived on adjoining sections. They had three boys, the two younger of which attended White Lake School.

Since this was Don's first year in school and being a totally "new" world to him, he didn't know quite how to react to a teacher in the classroom. In fact he thought it quite a hilarious place to be. Since, also, our grades shared the same classroom with him, I witnessed several occasions that were absolutely comical. One, I shall share here.

It seems that Don was talking aloud to a girl in the seat in front of him. The teacher but *never* permitted whispering or talking during classes. (Several classes were transpiring simultaneously, having the first, second, and third grades in the same room.) Miss Jackson, the teacher went over to Don and asked him to stop talking. Being his first couple of days in school, he had no idea what she was referring to and kept talking to the girl. Miss Jackson asked him to stand up. He did. She spanked him a couple of times cross the rear end. He thought that was quite funny and laughed about it in real amusement. Miss Jackson stood and glared at him, he kept laughing. She returned to her desk and sat down and resumed her class. Later, she told Mom and Dad of the event; all three got a huge laugh out of it. But all through life, Don was one to live on the positive side and see a laugh in most things, and, especially, when reminded of that day in the third grade at **White Lake School**.

CHAPTER 8

* * *

MEMORIES SO PRECIOUS

During the younger years of one's lifetime, it seems there are more memories which are more meaningful than others. It seems there are certain experiences that remain with us longer and stay more vivid in our minds. And, then, there are those experiences and events and people, those dreams we all have, those sweethearts, those heartbreaks and tears, and all those other things that affect us in so many un-describable ways. Then there are those times in our lives that we would do well to forget but can't. This chapter presents some of those things worth putting "pen to paper," so to speak.

Christmas time always was so special in my life. It was special in a much different way than it was for most people, I think. All those years while growing up in a homestead community, as I have iterated several times prior, we as individuals and as a family had none of the luxuries and finery of the more elite in the cities and other areas of prosperity. We were limited to what we could scrape out of the soil and to that which we could fashion from the materials at hand. This included clothing, food, transportation and the like. It included everything. The only items of luxury we possessed in our family was my mother's old Edison phonograph which provided our music until in the late 1930s when we purchased our new Airline radio from Ward's for $17.85. But there was much more to Christmas, its real meaning, and the closeness brought to the families during this season.

Yes, we would have a Christmas tree at Christmas time. The family traveled to the mountain where Dad would chop down a pinyon pine tree, and we would haul it home in the wagon; sometimes in the deep and driving snow. We would all work together making paper chains and popcorn (which we raised) chains strung on a string, and arrange them on the tree under the strict supervision of Mom who was an accomplished designer (in us kid's eyes, at least). Then on went the candle holders which held the candles in an upright position and would catch the hot wax as it ran down the burning candle. The candles were placed in the holders to be lighted at the proper time on Christmas day. Whatever homemade presents we had prepared in secret during the year, were placed under and on the tree for opening on Christmas morning bright and early, and I do mean bright and early!!

The same was done at the school. The teachers and the parents and students would take a day to decorate the school about a week before Christmas day. The walls were decorated with home-made garlands of paper and others of popcorn, pine cones and branches, wreaths made of trimmings from the tree, ribbon contributed by mothers' sewing boxes, and "paintings" done by us kids, master pieces to say the least!

Songs were practiced, skits were written by the teachers and rehearsed, and, finally, the time arrived for the parents to visit our class room to share with us Jesus' Birthday. A real celebration in which God was in our midst for we all felt Him and were greatly humbled by His presence. Yes, God was in our classroom. God was there. This was our celebration of the birthday of Jesus, and it was repeated each year, and was before the terrible and stupid law prohibiting religion in the schools.

There was no commercialization seen except for a couple of the more affluent families in the community who tried to show up we poor families and flaunt their expensive presents" Santa Claus" brought them. But we understood the situation and we were sad for them. We were sad for them because they knew not the meaning of Christmas and how it should be celebrated; as Jesus' Birthday. This was the day God brought Himself to us in a human body like ours to teach us and to die for us eventually. Yes, we were so happy to celebrate together and so humbled by His presence and so sad for those who didn't actually "feel" their love for Him in their hearts.

Yes, Christmas in my life has been a very important and heartfelt event. I am so glad I had the opportunity to be attending school during the times when God was permitted to be taught and worshiped in our public schools. It isn't a matter of one's having a right to NOT hear about God for fear what they might hear something that might conflict with their "beliefs." These people should be the ones to be *made* to hear about Him and His teachings. We have NO "right" to interpret His teachings for our own selfish convenience, but an obligation just to follow the rules He laid down, because the truth IS that we are the product of God's own handiwork, NOT our own handiwork! One must remember, also, that Jesus did in fact tell his disciples to go into all the world and teach everyone about his teachings, not to ask them whether they "wanted" to hear about them or whether they "agreed" with them. This argument could be used about arithmetic or English, or science subjects as chemistry, also. We attend school to learn the subjects and rules of conduct, not whether we agree with them and pick and choose the ones we agree with (Yep! I ended that sentence with a preposition, a no, no, but, then, this is *my* book, isn't it?).

Yes, Christmas and its meaning and the celebrations we had at home and school have molded my life and personality and made me able to truly be happy and grateful for those things, though meager, that were made available for me and for my personal successes. I have no regrets nor do I have envy for those who have much more than I. I am happy they have the comforts of life, but I am also saddened they might not truly feel what a true Christmas celebration is about.

Also, we were taught about our own country's government, its divisions, its houses of congress, the citizens' duties and privileges, and how it operates. We were taught these things in a subject called "Civics" from the fourth grade on through high school. We had to memorize all the presidents, their vice presidents, their sequential number, and the years of their tenure. These things aren't taught any more to this extent or at all in most schools, and is very evident when conversing with modern-day graduates. Nor is geography taught to the degree as it was then. Hardly anyone under the age of fifty at the date of this writing knows all the countries of the world, their states, their capitals, the principle industry, the population and those things pertaining to each of all the states, as we had to know in order to graduate from the eighth grade, not to mention completing a course or two in your own state's history. (Also, two years of a foreign language was required to graduate from Claunch High School, that little "one horse school" as city folks would refer to it, but can **they** equal the quality of education we received?) All this is so obvious when observing people participating in "trivia" contests and simple conversations. Such expensive schools our high taxes buy, and such uninformed, uneducated, and naive people graduating from them! As I have said and proved over and over again, "Educating students is NOT a function of the amount of money spent per capita, but a function of the knowledge and intelligence and ability of the teaching staff and the dedication they exhibit in implementing the transfer of that knowledge and EXPERIENCE to the student." Education and learning have, for millennia, been occurring among all levels of people, rich and poor alike. This "money" we all seem to hear that is "needed" is for the purchase of flashy and luxurious "teachers' toys" and flashy new buildings. Learning can happen anywhere from in a cave to the most ornate of palaces. One day, educators will be forced to exhibit more smarts in transferring knowledge than showing off their luxurious surroundings. This I see in the future and, therefore, predict. There are so many, many precious memories from those wonderful days of so long ago, those days which most "modern" folks refer to as "hard times" and days of so much suffering and poverty, and days of such hard work and days of no jobs. Actually, we folks who grew up during those times actually never had a clue that we were "poor" or were "starving" or were mistreated" any way. Actually we never found these things out until AFTER the Second World War was ended and people began having scads of money to throw around and began "comparing" that condition to the situation during the thirties. However, I treasure those years and the things I learned and all those wonderful experiences and all the loving and wonderful lifelong friends that were made, and some of which still live to enjoy our visiting each other.

But another vivid and wonderful memory is the closeness between people and between people and their farm animals. For example, there were our dear neighbors, the Schoonovers.

Thel and his wife Lena moved to the area and homesteaded just a mile and a half west of our place where the "broke" up the sod with plows and built a farm to call their home. They had two boys about my age and Don's age and we became close friends over the years to follow. It needs to be said here that no medical doctors or hospitals existed this side of Albuquerque, some 120 miles. This, quite simply means that folks had to do their own doctoring however best they could. Some folks had knowledge of health matters and diseases and fractures and so on, but most didn't.

The boys' names were Walker, the oldest, and Wilburn, the youngest. Winters sometimes could be very harsh. The winter of 1934 was no exception. Snow came down, sub-zero temperatures prevailed and much wood was fed to every heating stove. Houses had no heat at night time, and only several heavy quilts on every bed kept one warm enough to survive in some semblance of comfort.

Wilbur, being a bit more frail than most, began to succumb to the cold weather and less than warm nights and came down with double pneumonia. Well, as was the custom, then, the women folks prepared gallons of chicken soup from their own flocks, brought quilts and blankets and home remedies and sat the clock around with the Shoonovers. Some of the men folks busied themselves hauling new wood those 10, or so, miles from the mountains as others chopped the wood and kept the heating and cook stoves fired. Folks arrived and worked in shifts around the clock during the weeks of Wilbur's confinement. That was the unspoken law of the prairie it seemed, and to my knowledge only two persons died as the result of that kind of sickness in that area during the entire eighteen years I lived there until my departure to the Army. One was Mrs. Henrietta Spear, a Chiropractor from Michigan who had migrated to Claunch and opened a store with her husband who had been a grocer in their home town of Detroit. Mrs. Spear died during childbirth, but the baby survived and still lives I'm told, tho' I know not where.

Oh, yes, she, Mrs, Spear, died in a hospital in Albuquerque with her doctor and husband at her side.

The other person to pass away from a sickness was a dear little personal friend of mine who lived in the old Abrams place just west of our place. Yes, Wayne Talley was only nine years old when he, too, contracted pneumonia and died in Albuquerque. This touched me very deeply because Wayne used to catch a ride with me daily on my bicycle when we went to the rural mailbox (which was on the main road a half mile west of the Talley's house), and he never did wear a coat during cold weather. I would ask him about it, and he would answer, "I ain't got one." So I would unbutton mine and wrap it around both of us as he sat in front of me on the bike frame. The last time I saw Wayne was the week before his funeral when we rode to the mailbox together. Each time I visit the Claunch cemetery I go by his small grave and say a prayer. May he rest in sweet peace!

On a lighter note: The Galloway's were a family which lived some seven and a half miles to our west with whom we became not only well acquainted, but extremely good friends and neighbors. Mr. Galloway was a locomotive engineer for the Santa Fe Railroad, and, for many years ran the freight run from Belen to Vaughn. They owned a home in Belen where they lived most of the time, but they also homesteaded a section of land there in our area southeast of Gran Quivera. The children comprised William (Bill, the fiddler), Floyd, and Virginia (who had been afflicted with infantile paralysis early in life, later called polio). This was a family of good and religious people with no history of undesirable activities whatsoever. It was sad enough to see Virginia with her leg brace and crippled right leg which remained covered with long dresses when she was in public. We boys, however, grew up in her acquaintance and had no notions other than she was a perfectly normal girl and student and daughter to her parents. Floyd, on the other hand seemed to be a walking bag of bad luck waiting to happen. Such a nice well-mannered boy a bit on the slightly plump side, but one who always practiced good manners wherever he was, and he was well liked and had many friends. But, poor Floyd! Seems that most of what he tried turned into a bag of worms of one kind or another. I'll give an example.

His first job out of high school was one with a building contractor in Belen who built new construction and repaired old structures. Floyd was assigned to help install oak flooring in this new private home that was being built and was instructed to use the table saw to saw a few pieces of oak flooring to size to fit into a certain area of the dining room floor. Yes, I'm afraid you guessed it! It wasn't long after he started the project that the piece of flooring he was running through the saw slipped, and Floyd sawed off his index finger and thumb of his right hand. Yes, clean as a whistle. It fell into the sawdust bin beneath the saw. It did! He didn't even feel it, he said. Of course the contractor seemed more worried about it than did Floyd and wasted no time in rushing Floyd to the hospital there in Belen. There his hand was cleaned and stitched and bandaged. But the story doesn't end there.

A few weeks later Floyd complained that his finger was "sure getting tired" of being on top of his thumb. This kept on for a few more weeks and finally reached the point where he "couldn't stand it anymore." Well, now, in retrospect Floyd after having returned from the hospital, had been presented with his detached appendages (which were still attached to each other by the connecting tissue) which he straight away buried in the back yard in a shoe box. This "feeling" of tiredness had continued for several days and had reached the point of extreme fatigue on the part of Floyd's missing parts. Of course, he shared this situation with most everyone he encountered. I suppose he figured discussing it would help matters, in what way I have no idea. However, a neighbor lady related to him and his family that she had known of a similar thing happening years ago to someone she knew and swore that the feeling of the finger being tired was actually caused by the finger actually being on top of the thumb where it was buried. Far-fetched??

Well the skeptical Floyd went to the back yard and dug up the shoe box, opened the lid, and what do you think he saw?? You guessed it!!! The finger WAS, in fact, laying on top of the thumb in the box when buried. He, still not convinced, removed the finger from its perch and laid it alongside the thumb and re-buried it. Yep! That did it!

Poor Floyd!! Now he had another mystery to untangle. WHY! Nearest the doctor could figure, he said, was that the brain last knew that the finger was in that position when it was severed from the body, and the brain sent the message that fatigue was present, and when he moved the finger, the brain was re-trained to know it was no longer laying on top of the thumb. Impossible??? Who knows the reasons behind these things, but one could never convince Floyd it didn't happen.

No greater respect hath no man subsequently for a table saw than Floyd.

CHAPTER 9
* * *
MY INQUISITIVE AND INVENTIVE SIDE...

My Definition:

SCIENCE: The organized and totally impersonal Logical Investigative and analytical approach to the methods, procedures, and timing and all *other* dimensions used by God the Creator during His creation and operation of the entire universe, and all involved in it, in addition to the four dimensions we presently know and teach: length, width, height, and time.

I submit, also, that many other dimensions exist and are based entirely on God's own specific principles in which mass, as man likes to call it, but has never been properly and correctly defined by man. It is the method God uses to present Himself to man by utilizing earthly dimensions. When converted back to Heavenly principles, as in death, the energy returns to Heavenly dimensions where all four of the earthly dimensions are eliminated and are, therefore, rendered invisible to earthly beings without the slightest understanding by them! I, also, submit that the spirit and soul exist within these other dimensions where *only* energy exists. What man refers to as *mass* being energy spinning centripitaly so fast and tightly as to appear as solid. Therefore, it is my contention and reasoning that only one thing exists: *energy*! Forrest Newitt Easley

D own through the many years, all the way from my early childhood until the present time, I have continually been a person who was filled with great curiosity and inquisitiveness.

I have always had the great desire for learning, not just one particular subject, but any and all subjects. I have to qualify that by saying that from one time to another, the subject of curiosity probably would and did vary greatly. This proved to be a hazard to learning because I found myself in the middle of learning about one subject and suddenly would have a strong desire to delve into a totally different subject headlong without finishing the first. Many, many things got sidetracked because of this undisciplined action on my part. To this day, I must strive very hard and pay strict attention to more seriously schedule and finish things before heading into another undertaking, or, at least, be certain I can collectively finish all items at hand in a timely and reasonable and responsible manner.

Another facet of my makeup is the great ability and desire to analyze and alter, at least in my mind, the very basic philosophy by which most things have been and are done. An example of this would be as follows: Since birth, I suppose, I was taught not to be selfish in any manner because God teaches us to be unselfish in all things but to share. I was taught that the devil is the one that persuades people to think selfishly and collect worldly things unto ourselves. That being said, here is what bothers me no end. Sports. Yes sports! Take any sport as an example. The rules of the sport require everyone to acquire score points for themselves, to NOT let the opponent accumulate points. In other words, we are taught since early childhood to be "competitive" and always place ourselves in the winning position; at our jobs as well. In other words we are taught to be selfish and think of ourselves as the "winner" because we collect the most points or "things," and the most important person or team in a group. I honestly believe this to be grossly selfish, wrong, and to be totally immoral. So, instead, for example, of doing our utmost to "prevent" our opponent in a football game or baseball game from gaining points in order to accumulate the "most" points and, thus, "win" the game, (which makes each opponent "selfish" in trying to outdo the other). Perhaps we should rewrite the rules. Here is the example of one of those "un" selfish remedies I reasoned out.

Instead of the opponents working so hard to prevent each other from obtaining points, why not work equally hard trying to *give* each other points. The side having the fewer points would be considered the winner. This principle could be applied to all games, thus making them all non-selfish games. This principle could be applied, as well, even to our monetary system, thus making it non selfish in nature and, thus, eventually societies would become unselfish and acceptable to God Himself! These are but a couple of examples of the modifications in basic philosophies I have created in my mind in order to make our world a "good" world; a world like unto the Heaven we are taught to long for and to eventually see. However, the basis for MY thinking is that IF we continue the selfish thing, we absolutely will not measure up to our Creator's standards! Hmmmmmm. Food for great thought!!

But back to the topic at hand: As far back as I can remember, I recall being the "question box" as Mom called me. She would often become aggravated and frustrated with me for asking, "Why does this...," or, "Why does that do that?" I was constantly wanting to know "why!" Or "what!"

Then, too, if I could put my hands on an item of discard, or obsolescence, I immediately would disassemble it and reassemble it, then disassemble it again just to find out what made it operate. Clocks and watches were no exception. I'd say by the time I was eight or nine years old, I could fix a dollar watch or alarm clock as well as anyone. It seemed to me to be a simple little machine whose spring and gears and escape fork was just a simple device that would keep time if the bearings (pivots) weren't worn out from much usage or the spring wasn't broken. If this seemed to be the case, I would invent some way to "fix" the problem by studying the piece in question and either making a new one or repairing the old one until it would work again. There never was a "mystery" connected with any machine or device from MY viewpoint. There still isn't! All things have been constructed by "somebody" out there somewhere, and if they could build it, so could I! I have always looked at it that way, and have proven to myself (and to my father) that I could do just that. I have never been mystified by machines, whether electrical or mechanical, small or large. The human body is the same. I have always been quite curious about the entire human "machine" and all its functions and makeup. I have even gone so far as to study formal text books of anatomy and physiology and most of the texts required of a medical student, and I find them most interesting and informative. I think I would have made a great doctor because that has always been like a "first love" of mine. My wife, Marilyn, also tells me she shares the same feeling.

So technically, I find my major interests in all of nature and mechanics and physics and the solar system out there. Not only am I interested in those things, and find them of great interest, I apply myself to learning, every chance I have, everything I can possibly learn about them. Of course, I make certain the information I pursue and study is legitimate and not merely someone's opinion, which most of the time is not worth much in terms of real knowledge. Truth is, after all, the validity of something with respect to an unquestionably accurate and reliable basic source. In other words, truth is truly factual, and factual, by definition, is absolute forever. For example, the statement that the sun will rise tomorrow morning is a fact because it has been proven over and over again each day since the beginning of time itself. The basis for this supporting information comes from God Himself since He himself designed and created the sun and earth and the universe and has "programmed" things to function as He dictates. Other things that we (man) call "facts" are really not facts at all, but theories at best since they haven't been proven for a long enough period of time without failure. So I am very careful about categorizing things into either a hypothesis, a theory, or a fact (absolute truth). An example of an "untruth" is that the fraction 1/3 can be expressed precisely in decimal form. It cannot. (Contemplate: 0.33333333333333333333333333...ad infinitum.) There will always be a three at the end which there is still a small bit unaccounted for, even though it becomes very small, but never zero.

I have yet another belief which I truly believe is "nature's" mathematical base. I believe nature in all its universe and its philosophy is based on the concept of "base three." NOT to base ten as all present-day mathematics is organized by human thinking. In nature, no "zero" exists! Only in mans' minds and so-called "logic" does zero exist. By our own definition, the zero means it has NO value. It is considered and used in order to provide a vehicle by which the "base ten" philosophy of Mathematics might function and provide the "decimal system" of numbers. In digital philosophy, the zero allows one to imagine a function is "off" and the one allows the system to be "on."

In "base three" thinking, and in nature, there is no situation where "nothing" exists. Either it is matter, it is not matter but a "vacuum", but, at least, there is something, vacuum! So when one checks nature, things rarely occur in groups of "ten" but in groups of three and multiples of three and its related combinations and relationships. The new philosophy would be that one would relate numbers to each other instead of relating them to ten. Example: the numeral one could be stated as three less two, and the numeral nine would be considered as three plus two times three. Twelve would be three plus three times three, and fifteen is three plus four times three and so on ad-infinitum. ALL numbers and values would have absolute values using this philosophy. The base three idea would need to be the basic philosophy and the "base ten" idea trashed altogether! Observe the petals of a lily, the stars in Hercules' belt.

Another field of interest is research itself. Research in any field. I enjoy, thoroughly, developing ideas and ways and methods and rules and formulae. I also enjoying double-checking other scientists' claims, discoveries and inventions to determine whether I can improve upon them. This even extends into the medical field. I have very interesting conversations and discussions with my doctors and surgeons. This is quite satisfying and successful, in terms of diagnosis, to be able to converse as two learned persons, instead of one being "God" and the patient being a "dummy." But back to the idea of inquisitiveness and inventiveness.

Many times, even during my childhood, I recall situations where I "just HAD" to find out what made some machine "go" and also what it looked like inside. Just after we had moved into our new house that Dad built at Claunch, he had to store all the electrical things in the cellar ("basement" to city folks.). As I said much earlier, we had no electricity, nor did we have running water, nor did we have an inside toilet or sink or refrigerator! So all the things that were moved from Newton that could not be used at Claunch were stored in the cellar. This gave ME a great opportunity to "investigate" all the fine specimens which I had NO idea of just what they were other that a funny name Mom and Dad called them. I remember that funny thing called a "sweeper." Now, come on! I saw no broom on it, at least none that resembled the one Mom used to sweep the floor upstairs. All I saw was a little black brush inside of it when I turned it upside down. So I asked Mom and she explained to me that there was an "electric motor" inside that turned the brush 'round and 'round. I ran back down there and turned the brush 'round and 'round with my fingers. I could see how that would scratch the rug or floor and get the dirt off, but that "electric motor" was of quite a lot of interest. I peered through the openings in it and saw many other things in there, none of which I understood the least thing about. But guess what!! I looked around for a way to take it apart! Yes I did! I found my dad's old pliers and started work. I remember this as though it were yesterday. I was in "big time" work now. All else disappeared from my mind and all effort was applied to getting that motor apart. I must say here that most kids wreck things taking them apart, but I never had that tendency. I always wanted to take things apart without damaging them, but to discover the way to do it without any damage.

To tell the true fact of the matter, I think I wanted very much to not leave any tel-tale evidence I had been into the motor because of Dad's willingness and desire to "tan my hide" for touching any of "his" things. So ultimately, it taught me indirectly to be a very careful mechanic. On the one hand, I suppose I am grateful for that, and on the other hand, I suppose I was a naughty boy and deserved a lickin', (Psychology was never one of my favorite subjects because I profoundly can't and don't go along with all the so-called "reasons" and so-called "studies" which are totally meaningless, anyway, in terms of hard scientific proof and development of natural forces and reactions and character, but if it were a legitimate science, I would never apply it to the situation described above anyway. Common sense and respect resulting from fear of Dad's strap was a great teacher just as respecting God's teachings and Commandments for fear that if you don't you shall pay the consequences in hell!)

But, as to the motor, I managed to succeed in my total investigation of it with only one hitch. I remember that in putting the motor back together, I had a devil of a time getting the brushes back into their places. This was the first time I had ever even seen brushes, in fact I didn't know they were called "brushes" until years later when Dad and I were talking and he used that word. Of course, when he explained about them and what they were for and where they were used, a vision of my investigative experience in the cellar that day came into view, and I figured *that* was what those things were that I almost had to get help from MOM to re-install. And so that's how it went at first, and so I learned many things along the way. And, then, there were those light bulbs over there in that box all wrapped individually in newspaper!

Yes! To me, those light bulbs seemed so huge, and they were of several colors: blue, yellow, red, and sort of white, and clear ones too. Mom and Dad must have used them for Christmas lights in the Newton house somehow. But I liked the clear ones because I could see what was inside of them. I was totally fascinated with that little "spring" inside held up by those four little wires. But they looked different than the ones in the car headlights, the only "bulbs" I had ever seen that I could remember. I remember going out to the Model T Ford and looking into the headlights at those little bulbs. They were so small and different. I asked Mom what made the "big" ones work, and she told me something about we would have to live in "town" for them to work. I didn't understand this at all, and she didn't either, except for the fact we didn't have any "wires" coming to the house!

Then there was the matter of the "*garden hose.*"

Yes, the hose. It was beyond me. I remember looking into the end of it, into that hole that seemed to just disappear way down inside of that thing. The other end was the same! I was soft and round and black, but those metal things on each end made no sense to me at all. I could see no use for them to be on there at all, but I did discover that I could "screw" them together, one onto the other. But this still had me wonder why somebody made such a thing. This is the wonderful thing about small boys playing alone with their parents' things: discovery!

Now at first thought, one would take for granted that a very small boy on a farm in New Mexico would know all about a garden hose. Wrong!! Not I! Not my cousins! Not my friends! Nobody, but nobody had a garden hose, but, you guessed it, the Easleys! We had several! But you couldn't have proved by me just how they were to be utilized.

NO Sir! Up to this time, I had never had the courage to "ask" Mom about the matter. Fear? Maybe! But I did discover that I could sit on the coiled hoses and "work" on that "electric motor." I believe that I had taken that motor apart a dozen times after I learned its "secrets" during the first disassembly. Actually, the coiled hoses made a very nice "nest" to sit in and play (or just nap). Eventually, as I grew a bit older, I remember discussing the hoses with my parents whereby they explained the finer points of the purposes of their usage. As a result, I found myself subsequently pouring water into one end of the hose expecting it to run out the other end. Wow! What magic! I could imagine myself being like the people in "town" and go around watering something about the place, just what, I have no idea because we had no grass or flowers or any of the other things Mom spoke of which they had in Newton. Instead, I would just follow bugs and lizards and spiders and "water" them instead, and play at this new discovery for hours wasting untold amounts of Mom and Dad's precious water which they had to haul in a wagon for miles. What great fun. What great memories! What great "truths" I shared with Mom and Dad in later years.

Dad was somewhat of a curious person also. Even though he had only a ninth-grade formal education, he had self-educated himself to the point he was quite a brilliant and well-informed and well-read individual. His interests included many areas of expertise from mathematics to electronics, to law, to mechanics, and to religious history, to railroading, to blacksmithing. Because of all these interests and more, he had back in the twenties become very interested in the newly developing "radio" industry and the idea that one could build their own radio set from parts available in "dime stores" all over the country. So he paid a visit to Kress's and bought a book on building your own set and all the parts necessary to do so. These included one type O1A radio tube, a grid leak, a grid leak condenser, a tuning condenser, a rheostat for adjusting the filament voltage, earphones, hookup and coil winding wire, and miscellaneous other hardware items he thought he needed to build a cabinet to put his radio into. He had built this set in Newton before we came to New Mexico. He was so pleased with its performance that a short time later, while still in Newton, he decided to build a two-tube set that two people could listen to simultaneously. I bring this up because it sparked my interest in the same subject: radio!

Money being so scarce, Dad had never bought the necessary "B" batteries to set up the radio in the new home at Claunch. Times were much too hard during the beginning years on the homestead for him to afford them, so the radio just sat on the shelf in the so-called "bathroom" which was serving only as a store room and pantry, so to speak. Curiosity and the burning desire to get that radio down and look inside it was getting the better of me, for sure. But Dad had warned me well NOT to touch that radio for any reason. But under greater and greater pressure and pleading. He gave in. He reluctantly got it down, and opened the lid.

Wow! Was I impressed! He had wound all those three large "coils" himself, and he had constructed every one of the strange-looking things I was gazing at with jaw dropped in awe! The first thing I wanted to do was to make one for myself. I wanted to make one too! "Will you teach me how?" I asked. So he did. He dug out his instruction book and sat me in his lap and we read it completely through.

(It was one of the few times I remember sitting on Dad's lap for any reason; a thing I had always longed to do, but never seemed to be a thing he wanted to do. I had always longed for my father's arms about me and goodnight hugs. I had always imagined just how warm it must be to be cuddled up to him in the cold of a winter's night in front of the roaring potbelly stove...sound asleep. But we weren't close, never had been, nor were we ever to be. I was an "accident." I was eight. Mom, my best friend, explained this when I reached age twenty as I shed my tears of sadness on her ever loving shoulder one day while visiting her at her day nursery. They're both gone now and I miss them terribly!)

Dad read the book and explained it to me and I learned every word in that little book. I still remember most every word of instruction in it. I still picture the diagrams and can visualize the picture of the placement of all the parts after construction. Of course, it was a very small booklet and didn't comprise many pages, either, but my interest was very keen and my memory good. Dad had collected many extra radio parts over those years, and told me of them. That did it! He got the parts out of their storage place and I was in business. I procured the boards from an old apple box to use to make a small cabinet and a mounting board to mount the parts on, and another to use as a terminal strip which to connect the batteries and the antenna and ground and the ear phones. I could hardly wait. I did the work all myself. Now for batteries! The "A" battery was the car battery from the old truck. It provided the 6 volts to light up the filament of the O1A tube. As it turned out, our neighbor, Finis Jones, had just bought new batteries for his radio and I thought he might give me the old ones. I asked, and he did! He dropped them by and Dad and I connected up my new creation. I relied on Dad because there was a "secret" way to connect the "A" battery and the "B" battery so as to provide "bias" to the tube. Dad explained that relationship to me for future reference.

A long wire was connected to the antenna coil and strung to a fence post some hundred feet away. The other side of the antenna coil was connected to a rod we drove into the ground just outside the window where the radio was located. Dad had me pour water around the ground rod to, "help make better connection to the earth," he explained. Dad turned on the set, and I erupted with the same squeal that emanated from the set's earphones as Dad adjusted the feedback with the regeneration knob. "Let me! I want to do it. Please?" I asked. He did. It worked! I was the most thrilled boy in the world, I just knew it.

The old "B" batteries still had enough energy in them to operate my radio, and I sat for hours listening to that radio set, and, since I longed for closeness with him, it pleased me no end to hear Dad say to me, "Forrest, can I listen to the news on your radio?" "Alright, Daddy." (I called him daddy back then.)

As I grew older, the breadth of my curiosity also increased, as did my reasoning and logic and wisdom, for a young boy, that is. As I have mentioned previously, the depression brought with it the need to survive as best one could, and if one desired or needed anything else, they had to give some thought to either doing without it, or earning the money to "buy" it (almost an impossibility), or getting busy and build the item of desire. So we, therefore, being used to "making" our things, did just that. So with that preface, in 1934 at my age ten, we found ourselves without a car battery with which to operate the "radio" I had built earlier, and, further, without an operating car with which to "charge" that battery we didn't have in the first place. This was of great concern to me because I had grown so accustomed to that radio and listening to *Jack Armstrong* and *The Lone Ranger and Tonto* that I began to seriously consider ways I could resolve that problem. We had several old worn out car batteries sitting around the place which had long past given up the ghost. But upon looking at them, I figured that since they each had three separate water filler caps, there had to be three separate parts inside the battery that were connected together. I could see the lead connector bars on top of the batteries. So I thought maybe all the "insides" (as I called them) might not all be bad in all the batteries, so I dug out the tar on top of the batteries and sawed the lead connectors in two with a hack saw and proceeded to remove all those "cells" as Dad wanted me to call them. I did. I also made Mom quite upset with me, *and* I learned a great lesson. I found out that the "water" in there wasn't water at all. It ate holes right through those precious clothes of mine, and Mom slightly lost her sweet disposition, to say the least.

After the dust settled, so to speak, and a few days had passed, Dad showed me how to handle this stuff he referred to as "sulfuric acid" without hurting myself (and my clothes) in the process. I proceeded to check each set of these battery sections to see if they were "good" or "bad." I could see some were very dirty and clogged up with gray "dirt" and some weren't. So I selected three "good" ones and washed them off with water (Dad said to use only rain water), and assembled them back into a battery case. But how to charge them... a real problem. AH HAH!!!! It came to me. I ran to the work shop and took a good look at the hand-cranked drill press we had there. YES! It will work.

To the home - made tractor Dad had built and had quit using and had parked behind the shop I went with wrenches in hand. I removed the generator from that 1927 Chevy engine and quickly took it into the shop and held it up over the drill press and lined up the drive belt pulley with the flywheel of the drill press. My vision was for real! All I needed was a steel band around the generator to fasten it to the vertical 2 x 6 board the press was mounted on. A search of the junk pile resulted in just the right thing, and I was in business. Dad helped me shape it and drill the holes for screws and make a belt from leather.

I soon learned that a 15-minute turn at cranking that drill press with ALL my might and sweat, that we could run the radio one night on the battery thus charged. The amount of sweat and huffing and puffing was adjusted upward to the point of having a radio for a week between charges. Not bad, but excellent exercise! I also learned a valuable principle which I much later in life studied in college physics: To place electrical energy into the battery, I had to put OUT much more physical energy in the form of WORK with which the mechanical energy was converted into electrical energy through changing the chemicals in the battery. WOW! Complicated stuff, back then!

But, as we know, things never remain the same or constant in nature, especially the human mind (in a "normal" person, that is).

One of my all-time favorite magazines was ***Popular Mechanics*** . I would read and re-read each issue, ads and all! The entire magazine. In one particular issue, I ran across an ad for "Instructions" to build your own wind generator machine. FREE! As you probably are guessing, this was of great and immediate interest to me. I sent for it and counted the days until its arrival. I could hardly wait, and each day seemed to get longer until...one day it arrived in the mail, a brown envelope with a few typed pages of instructions how to "rewind" a Model "T" Ford generator to make it charge at a much slower speed, and a drawing of how to make a wooden "base" and tail and a "Propeller" to turn the generator at "high speed." What a find!

We had the generator from the old Ford and I wasted no time disassembling it and taking the old wiring off the armature. Rewiring wasn't that bad because the instructions had good pictures of how to do the new windings. No problem. Neither was the propeller because I liked to work with wood and had built a nice little radio table (which I still possess) and had finished it nicely with a home-brew walnut stain and varnish as a 4-H project. So in about a week of loving effort, I had a brand new "wind charger," and I never had to crank that drill press again, except to drill holes in steel in later years.

These are but a few of my early life's experiences which served to set the mood and mode of later life's experiences and the direction my life has taken. I have never had anything but a desire to do good things for both myself and others. Also, I have never had a desire, nor would I permit myself to lean toward dishonesty, corruption, disgrace, sinful living, rowdiness (which I see in most young people, both male and female, of current times). Also, I was taught to have respect for everyone, especially those "older" than I, and everything both animate and inanimate, because all things and all life are of Gods doing, and nothing did I create, nor could I create it, because God Himself reserves THAT power unto Himself alone! Yes I truly am curious and inquisitive until this day, just days after my 77th birthday. I have actually, believe it or not, truly lost friends because of my refusals to yield to their short comings and ways, but, then, I have made even better ones, although fewer, by being unyielding. But the best friend I have made is my loving God and, then, my next best friend is my loving Wife, Marilyn.

CHAPTER 10
* * *
MY HIGH SCHOOL SENIOR YEAR

Just as the farming season was winding down in 1941, an almost new dark green 1940 Ford deluxe sedan pulled up to our place and stopped. Out in those parts of the country, everyone was familiar with every car in the area, and this car was a stranger! Strange cars far out in the country were suspect and figured by the natives to be some sort of hustlers from the city out to make a quick buck off the poor innocent homesteaders. Strangers usually were not welcome, for sure! However, to our pleasant surprise, this time these suspicions were unfounded. These were not strangers, but relatives who had been fortunate enough to purchase a new car and we hadn't become aware of it until it drove up to the house.

It turned out to be a very dear friend and shirt tail relative of Dad's. It was Mrs. Hagee, the 81-year-old mother of Dad's sister's husband "Scott". When we saw who it was, we hurried toward them to greet them as they opened the car doors to get out. Hugs and handshakes were exchanged and a hello for us kids. Uncle Scott and Aunt Lena were the ones I mentioned earlier who had built the restaurant in Hollywood, New Mexico, near Ruidoso. We called her Mrs. Hagee because we, for life of us, couldn't remember her first name...I still can't! In fact, in those days, if a person was "older" than you, they were to be called "Mister" or Missus" and, therefore, actually I don't believe we ever knew her first name. Mrs. Hagee couldn't drive a car, so she depended upon her grandsons, mostly, to drive her wherever she had to go. So this day it was "Budge's" turn at her wheel. Budge was the nickname someone had stuck Uncle Scott's oldest son, Scott, Jr. with. Just where they came up with that nickname, I'll never figure out. Naturally, we were tickled to see them and invited them into the house. Mom made lemonade from lemons we just by chance happened to have as a result of our recent trip to the store. We had no ice for it, nor ice box nor refrigerator (remember?), but the cold rain water from the cistern served the purpose very well. After a usual amount of "catching up", the adults settled down to the matter at hand. Dad, evidently, had written to her pertaining to the possibility of me staying at her house in Tularosa, some 100 miles away to the south, so I could attend my senior high school year there. As it turned out, the answer was affirmative and I was to be Mrs. Hagee's driver in return for my board and room. Wow! We had never owned a new car before except for the 1923 Model T Ford which we had when we moved from Newton. But I had little memory of that car since I was only about two years old. Our car at the time was a '35 ford sedan which I regarded about the very latest. Was I ever behind the times! Now I was going to be the driver of that "new" 1940 Ford! I could hardly wait, but at the same time I was very nervous about it! It drove like a dream! It didn't rattle! It rode so smooth! Also, it smelled so wonderful inside. I had never smelled a new car before, and I would contemplate for the longest time just what made it smell that particular way. I loved to just sit there in the car and take in that essence into my nostrils and savor it. Poor country kid I was...so ignorant of so many things of that big world out there, and yet so wise.

It was during the last few days of August, just a few days before school was to start. Dad and Mom and Don drove me to Tularosa with a sea trunk filled with my necessities. I even took along my violin which I had received on my fifth Christmas. Since there were no music teachers this side of Albuquerque, Mom, an accomplished pianist, began teaching me to play the violin as soon as it was given to me that Christmas morning. I took to it right away, and I responded fine...for a few years. Other things began to edge their way into my life and the violin began to take a back seat. So I thought that this would be an ideal time to take it with me and take lessons at school, because the Tularosa school system had a wonderful music program, and I was going to certainly take advantage of it.

School started and I was surrounded with hundreds of strange students. Now, strangers were always hard for me to meet. I most likely was one of the most timid kids ever to walk on two legs. I would walk a long ways out of the way to avoid a stranger for no particular reason, but I just didn't like to meet strangers. I was now in a situation where I could not avoid them. Everyone was a stranger! However, I did have one new friend, so to speak. That was Mrs. Hagee's grandson Jim Lackey whom I had met a while before. The Lackeys lived about two miles southwest of Tularosa and had a nice little farm out there and a wonderful garden. I remember Mrs. Hagee had me drive her out there every couple of days to gather a few things from the garden...my first introduction to that very slippery boiled okra!! That's the day I learned to hate boiled okra! But the watermelons and tomatoes made up for it and all was well with the world.

Well! NOT QUITE! I had gotten settled into school and all classes were great, especially music. However, I never even started the long-planned violin lessons. Why? Because the band teacher needed an E-flat Alto horn player. So guess who didn't have the courage to say NO! I did learn and did play the horn. It was quite simple compared to the violin, I thought. But as it worked out, much to my later regret, neighbors down the street in Tularosa had a son who was learning to play the Spanish guitar. Mrs. Hagee and I would drive over there and visit with them on occasion. Their son could actually play quite well and could sing while he accompanied himself with the guitar. Those western ballads sounded extremely good to me. They sounded so good that I began hankerin' to learn some of them. One Saturday morning while I was killing time strolling around, I stopped in at the only second hand store in town to look around just to see what I could see. Ah Ha!! There it was! A guitar! Wow, now I could be a cowboy singer too! You guessed it, I asked the store keeper whether he would consider trading the guitar for my "brand new violin". Well, after some humming and hawing, he decided to trade with me, and I ran home to get my violin.

I ran into the house and reached under my bed and took hold of the handle and slowly pulled it from under the bed. Something came inside me to handle it gently. I had always taken very good care of it. I dusted it regularly and polished its wood and kept it in tune. I just put off my practicing, that's all. Oh, I could play it after a fashion, even a classical piece or two. I remember Humoresque was a piece I liked particularly well and had learned it.

But now was the time to make a change. As I walked toward the second hand store a distance of about a mile or so, I gradually slowed down to slow walk and noticed the urge to rid myself of the beautiful violin for a second hand guitar, which I knew nothing about, was becoming just a faint glimmer. But how was I to back out on a deal? I had made a deal with the store keeper. Actually, I had kind of pushed the deal. No. I had to go through with it now, otherwise I thought I would be a person that couldn't be depended upon. So I turned into the door and laid my beautiful violin on the counter and bid it "goodbye." A tear almost came into my eye, but I couldn't let it be seen by this man. After all, I am a grown man now; I was 16.

My "new " guitar never even had a case, but I made excuses and told myself I would find one for it soon. In the corners of my very being I was very sad. I never ever felt happy about this transaction, even until this day. It was a gift from my parents on my fifth Christmas. I felt they never approved and were hurt, but would never let me know it. But many years later Mom let it slip and asked whether I had ever gone back to see if they still had my violin. Then I knew. Yes, I have made several trips back to see whether it was there. No, it has a new home somewhere and I know its wood is being polished and its case is being dusted and it is being kept in tune by its new master.

I did learn to sing and accompany myself and did it very well, however. I remember that Mrs. Hagee's place was narrow and very deep. In fact, the front of property was situated on Hagee Avenue, on the south, and extended north where the back of the property joined the main highway. This was a distance of about 600 feet, as I remember, and had a quince tree located dead center of the property. I mention this because this quince tree was quite large and provided the only real shady place where I could "practice" learning to play my newly-acquired guitar. This was very important to me because I was extremely bashful and shy. There was no way I would allow any person to hear

me practice. I just was very self-conscious about letting anyone hear me
play until I considered myself good and accomplished at whatever I was
doing. So I spent many hours out under the quince tree with my new
guitar and singing *Red River Valley* and *The Maple On the Hill*. But those
hours of practice and privacy gave me the confidence and experience to
finally agree playing the songs for Mrs. Hagee. But with senior classes
and other activities to deal with, I never really got to practice as much
as I wanted. Actually, I had to set the guitar aside temporarily and take
care of the necessary items first

Attending school at Tularosa High School was indeed a great change
from Claunch High School. First was there were a about 700 students,
and I knew only one of them! This was good for me, though, because it
helped rid me of some part of the shyness I had. Next I had many choices
of classes to take as electives, no electives at Claunch. So, as electives,
I took band, and I took Library science, and I took Business Law. Yes,
I learned to play the E-Flat Alto horn! There were no opportunities
to play the violin or guitar, however. But I was very pleased with the
situation as far as the school and its classes were concerned. However,
there was a very personal and serious problem which I never verbally
shared with anyone until many years later when I shared it with Mom.
This was a very embarrassing situation which I had no control over
at all, none! And I knew in my heart that no one even cared about
my embarrassment or feelings of isolating myself from everyone else
because of it. I remember one of the senior boys took me aside one day
after school and acted as if he wanted to talk to me, but he never did say
anything important about anything. I just concluded he lost his nerve
and just couldn't tell me that my feet smelled. Yes, they really did!

You understand! I truly had a problem! But, I had no control over
it, nor did I have a solution to it. The reason was this: As I have said all
the way through this writing, we were poor on our homestead. We had
no money to speak of, certainly not enough to buy new shoes for me
to wear at school. The style there in the city school was dress oxfords
for the boys. They were very expensive, and were way beyond our
budget. So Dad had given me his old dress shoes which he had worn
for at least ten years. They were sweaty and smelly and deformed and
I hated them, but they were all I had. The weather in Tularosa is hot

and humid in the fall, and my feet were always hot and would always sweat and became smelly as were Dad's. How embarrassing! Yes, and I knew it was embarrassing to all the other kids in all the classes. It was so very hard to have to look forward to classes each day and know what embarrassment lay ahead.

But I knew what the problem was and I knew what that fellow student wanted to tell me. I also knew that bathing and washing my feet and changing my socks daily had no effect upon the problem. So it became harder and harder to go to classes. Oh, my grades were excellent and all that, but I just couldn't face all those kids any more, not even for a minute. Finally, I decided to end it all. I would leave school and return home to Claunch before graduation. I just could not stick it out and suffer all the anguish of embarrassment anymore. So I began preparing for my clandestine return trip home.

However, there was another thing that was heavy on my mind too. I was quite fond of a certain young lady in my class, and she of me. How was I to leave her? She had never, no never let the "foot condition" affect her or our relationship. She was very nice and I knew she was a good person and I liked her a lot. So I asked God to guide me. I think He did. I got this urge to walk after school to the train depot which was a mile west of town and just sit and watch the trains arrive and leave. I did this. I did this until evening. Then, this freight train pulled into the depot and, unlike the others, stopped with the middle of the train even with me. A n empty boxcar with opened doors was directly in front of me. I began to think that I could get into this car and ride it to Carrizozo and get off. There I could hitch hike home, another 45 miles north. I looked up and down the right-of-way to see whether anyone was watching, but I was afraid of getting caught and arrested for trespassing. The train remained stopped for about an hour or more until another train approached from the north and passed on the main line and kept on traveling south. The engineer of the steam locomotive on the parked train gave his whistle signal and the train began to move slowly back onto the main line to continue its journey north. I had this strong urge to climb into this empty car and go home! I did! So I began to run alongside the car and managed to jump up and with a great amount of struggling I got into the car safely. Alas!! I looked up and what did I see? I saw another person already in there. I was startled to say the least. He was sitting against the forward end of the car very quietly and very still. He was a hobo and I was frightened clear down to my shoes! What had I gotten into? Was I going to be killed? Those were the questions I remember that came into my mind. But he spoke first and was very friendly and tried to find out what my problem was and where I was headed. Then he gave me a few pointers about how to avoid the "Dicks", the railroad detectives who would throw you off the train instantly. He was a Negro man and a very courteous and kind person to me. We arrived in Carrizozo about nine thirty that night and the train slowed down at the railroad yard limits which were two miles south of town. The other fellow told me to stay away from the open doors until the train came to a stop. This was because the detectives had a light on either side of the train that shined through the cars to see any hobo that might be in the car, then get them out and arrest them. So we hid in a forward corner of the car, and, then, immediately after the train stopped, we exited on the far side and escaped under about three parked trains next to ours. I ran and ran and ran until I was out of town and hid in the sage brush. I remained there until about midnight until I figured it was safe to re-enter town and look for a free place to sleep. I was extremely cold curled up under that sage bush trying to go to sleep, and I had no coat. So I gave up the idea of sleeping out of doors and made my way back into town and decided to try the local hotel lobby. I figured the desk clerk would be in bed by this time and I would be able to curl up on the couch in the lobby until time for him to come to work at about five the next morning. I did manage to sleep sporadically, but I periodically would awaken and look all around fearing the worst, that I would be spotted and tossed out in the cold. But I did get some rest and left early in the morning after washing up in the public rest room in the hotel. I headed north walking up Highway 54 without breakfast. No money, no eat!

The early morning air was brisk and just above freezing. I walked fast in an effort to keep warm, but the faster I walked, the faster the created breeze passed my body, and the colder I became. I was trying hard to acclimate my mind to the long 45-mile walk home, but I was praying to God that He would let the sun warm me just a little, at least to the point of being tolerable. I walked several miles and noticed myself observing the thousands of yucca plants (called "bear" grass in those parts) just to pass the time. It wasn't that I had never been over that road before, because I had. I had been on that road dozens of times over the years, and I knew it like the back of my hand, every mile of it! But the yucca seemed a bit taller than usual, then I remembered that I was at the moment not in a car, but walking. I had never walked the road before. The yucca is the state flower of New Mexico and there were literally thousands of them surrounding me at the moment. A beautiful sight to behold for sure with the early winter morning sun backlighting it so beautifully.

I was suddenly awakened from my day dream by an approaching school bus from behind. I turned and recognized the bus as that owned by Mr. Collins from Claunch. He pulled up alongside me and opened the door and invited me to get in and he would give me a ride home. God certainly had been listening to my plea, for sure. We had a nice visit on the trip home, since we hadn't seen each other for about a year, and we had to catch up on all the happenings and current gossip. Mr. Collins' school bus was new and one of the first "factory made" school busses to be used at the Claunch school. My feet were very cold having walked several miles on that frozen highway, not to mention not having a coat to wear, and I certainly felt compelled to sit as close as possible to the bus's wonderful heater. This was a circumstance and experience to remember, for sure!

The folks were, to say the least, very surprised to see me get out of that school bus that morning when Mr. Collins dropped me off at our place. I had a lot of explaining to do of why I was home and not in school. I never did, as I said before, tell of the smelly-shoe situation. I just iterated that I was unhappy with going to school there in Tularosa, and decided to return home. Dad saw my situation and also knew I was most serious about it and made plans to leave right away to drive to Tularosa to retrieve my possessions. I would finish out my senior year at Claunch High School. This I did, almost. As it turned out, Dad and I, who never were very close anyway, had a disagreement just before graduation time and I left home. I obtained a job on a cotton farm in Las Cruces, New Mexico. It was easy to get that job because the owner of that farm, Mr. Lavell, also owned a farm near Claunch. This was the end of me living at home with my parents. The following summer was very hot, the work was very hard, and I got very homesick for my mother, my brother, and my little sister. So, after a few months, I decided to return to Claunch and work on Mr. Lavell's other farm, but I never returned home except to visit the folks.

CHAPTER 11
* * *
INTRODUCTION TO REALITY

The year of reality had arrived! The year had come when I had to face the real world. The cold, cruel world was staring me in the face, and I felt I could handle anything. Yes, I figured I was ready and that I knew as much as the best of men. So I decided I would work hard and build a good reputation which all men would accept as outstanding. I would be known as a very hard-working and honest and sincere person who was willing to work endless hours to do my work and make it a real asset of my employer. But even more, I envisioned myself as my own person in the distant future and planned my own entrepreneurship as soon as possible. These were my goals! These turned out to be my permanent goals which I have chosen to follow ever since. Some deviation has occurred, of course, but for the most part, I have followed those goals which I established for myself at age 16 in the year 1940.

As a result of this vow, employers have always respected my efforts and my work and my attitude and my loyalty all of my life. Of course, I have run into a couple or three employers who were out and out jerks and did their best to cheat and discredit me, but on the whole, things have always worked out very well in those regards. But, as I began my "career," I was employed on the Lavell Farms as a farmer's helper. The farm I worked on mostly was located to the southeast of Gran Quivera, New Mexico some five miles, just at the boundary of the prairie and the Utah Juniper timber forest. The house was situated at the edge of the trees, and the fields were all in the open prairie grassland. The fields were two, and next to each other, and had been broken up for farming some ten years prior by a lady "Holiness" preacher, (Monty Turner, sister to Jones Turner who owned the main store and blacksmith shop in Gran Quivera) but which had grown up in weeds and needed a lot of revitalization work.

The man who was the lead person in charge of the farm was named Ed Bogges and was hired because of his great talents as a farmer. His background went back into Oklahoma and Texas where he was well respected as a sharecrop farmer and, although without a formal education, he was excellent manager of small sharecropped farms. I considered myself very fortunate to be able to work under him as his helper. We made a good working pair and he taught me well. But let's begin at the beginning.

In the beginning as a young man of sixteen being on my own, I had nothing. I had only a couple of pairs of khaki pants, a khaki shirt, a couple of blue chambray shirts, two or three pairs of cotton socks, a straw hat, an old belt of my dad's, a couple of handkerchiefs, and one pair of long underwear, and an old pair of work shoes, and the oxfords. Moving was very easy for me because it was just a matter of only one brown paper grocery sack and properly folded items inside. The other possessions of mine stayed with my parents and comprised the unnecessary items such as my guitar and some books and childhood toys which I greatly treasured but had absolutely no use for at the moment, even though I had planned to retrieve them should I would ever own a home somewhere sometime.

So when I went to work with Ed, I just took my paper sack of clothes and walked the seven miles to the Lavell Farm. Ed put me up as one would a person who wasn't a member of the family, but a hired hand or hobo. He had no extra room as people do now. He had no empty out building either. What he did have was an old frame farm house with a living room, a bedroom, and a kitchen. The cistern was just on the outside of the back door a few feet to the right as you exited the house. The bedroom was utilized by their daughter, Irma, where she had her bed and a wire strung across one corner of the room which she used to hang up her clothes. They were covered with a sheet to keep the dust off them.

The front room was a dual-purpose room. It was a living room which contained a few unmatched cane-bottom chairs, an upholstered "easy" chair, (which was referred to as the "easy cheer"), a small ratan card table, a new battery - powered console Philco radio with a Rayo kerosene mantle lamp sitting on top. Also, and beside the radio, next to the wall in front of a double-hung window was a wood heating stove. Their bed was in the southwest corner of the living room, and their dresser was at the foot of their bed. Likewise, a wire was strung across one corner of the room and provided a place to hang their clothes which were also covered with a sheet. A Victrola console phonograph sat beside the head of their bed next to the front door. The floor was unfinished well-worn pine lumber which was kept swept daily and clean as a pin.

As was obvious, there was no place for me to reside in the house, nor even outside, as such! So I made do. I had, long years previous, learned not to complain or to "want" luxury. So, I stayed where I could, where it was safe from rattle snakes. But usually, I could either sleep in Ed's car or in the upholstered chair in the living room next to the radio. But I was uneasy there because of the proximity to Ed and Evie's bed. So, I spent much time outside somewhere. Each night I just knew in my heart that Mom was thinking of me some miles away because I could "feel" it. I knew she loved me and prayed for me regularly. This, I am positive, is how I got me from one day to the next.

But work time came early. We would rise at four in the morning, and Ed would go to milk the cow, and I would go out and start the tractor and let it warm up while we had breakfast which Evie and Irma had cooked while we were outside doing the morning chores. Most breakfasts usually were about the same. They consisted of home-grown meat and eggs, usually scrambled, and hot biscuits and red-eye gravy. Sometimes they had white cream gravy and sometimes they had fried eggs. Meat varied from bacon to ham to sausage to steak to venison (when the neighbor could provide it). Very hot, very strong coffee was made in a blue tapered enamelware coffee pot which boiled on the back of the wood cook stove. Ed and I usually ate heartily and drank our second cup of coffee, then rose to begin our work outside.

During the spring season, we had spring plowing to do. This included planting the corn, barley and the bean crop. Our total acreage amounted to slightly under 500 acres which was divided into 50-row strips each of beans, and corn, and a hundred-foot-wide strip of barley. This was repeated over and over across the fields. Then the following year, crops were rotated onto different strips. We used two tractors which allowed us to finish the work quickly so that one of the tractors could be hauled to Las Cruces to the other farm to work in the cultivating of cotton and the mowing and raking of the alfalfa hay there.

Summer work was usually heavy, at least until the crops were laid by in August. Cultivating of the beans and corn was necessary to loosen the soil and to remove any weeds, and to work the soil up around the plants. Barley never required any cultivating unless it was planted in rows (as opposed to being broadcast planted). If it was planted in rows, we had to cultivate it similarly to the corn and beans. This made more work for us, but the yield was greater, also.

In the fall, we were faced with harvesting all the crops except the barley which had been harvested in late July and August. The beans were first to ripen and had to be cut with a bean harvester and windrowed with a side-delivery rake in preparation for the combine to thresh them. The corn, of course, had to be handpicked and thrown into a wagon pulled by horses. I explain all this because for two of us to handle 500 acres of these crops was a real undertaking. The main tractor was a new International Farmall "H" and would handle two rows at a time during listing, planting, and cultivating. It was used to pull the combine also. The other tractor was a large Minneapolis Moline and would handle four rows. But the Farmall "H" was used also on the cotton farm for the reason that it was easier to transport the 167 miles on the old 1934 Chevrolet ton-and-a-half truck. This old truck was used also to haul the farm produce to the El Paso markets in the fall. These trips were ones that indelibly imprinted themselves into our memories forever.

The old truck had seen better days, indeed, and it had never been coddled. Even so, it was still unbelievably reliable. In fact it had always been used hard and somehow always managed to hang together under those arduous and grinding trips over the Organ Mountains which were located to the west of the White Sands National Monument, and had to be crossed to reach our first destination at Berino, New Mexico, the location of the second farm and the owner's home. The roads for the most part were graded, gravel roads corduroyed from much use and lack of maintenance, just barely wide enough to allow two cars to meet and pass each other if the drivers exercised a bit of care in doing so. With those heavy loads of about five tons on that one-and-a-half-ton truck, tires were a big problem, too. One could consider himself very lucky, indeed, to complete the trip without a blowout. It is also worth mentioning that if one did have a flat tire for any reason, the only way to pump it up after it was repaired there on the spot, was with a hand tire pump. In order to pump the required 85 pounds of air pressure into a truck tire, one had to pump several hundred full strokes on the hand pump. This assumes that the pump was in good shape, which normally didn't apply.

I remember, too, that this was about the first year that Chevrolet trucks had factory-installed hydraulic brakes. However, in this extremely dusty part of God's world, those brake cylinders never stood up very long before needing the master cylinder cups replaced. So was the case with this old vehicle. The brake fluid leaked out almost as fast as one could pour it in, for it required very great foot pressure on the brake pedal to control those very heavy loads on those steep downgrades even when the gears were also used. Because of this, it became too costly to keep buying regular brake fluid. So we decide to use water instead. It worked great, but we had to keep a 5-gallon can of water sitting on the floor next to the shift lever. We just left the filler cap off the master cylinder, located just under the floor near the driver's right foot, so the passenger could keep the cylinder filled with that precious water.

So my first year on my own was a very hard one, and one filled with experiences which I shall never forget. My salary was one dollar per day because I ate with the family. Had I furnished my own meals, I would have gotten one and a half dollars per day. This was standard pay in that area at the time. However, a couple of years after the advent of World War II, wages went up to five dollars per day.

As the first year drew to a close, the weather also drew colder, but our work outside continued. The beans were sold and the ears of corn were brought in and piled in huge piles ready for the corn sheller. Ed spent his time doing the fall listing (furrowing) of all row-crop fields while I was assigned the task of shucking the ears of corn in preparation for shelling it. The weather grew colder, and my clothes grew thinner, and I resorted to my long underwear and two pairs of socks. The old shoes grew thinner, and the snow came down, the wind blew, and the nights grew longer, and more gunny sacks were added to my bed, and I thanked God Almighty for my blessings!

Work continued. Finally the corn was all pulled and stacked and Ed's days at the domino games on those cold days grew longer and more frequent. My work continued because I got paid by the day at work. He got paid by the month. So cold days, snow days, or windy days, or cold windy-snowy days, I worked outside. Gunny sacks also made good wraps for my shoes to keep my feet warm. I think one of the best things to help me through the cold days, except for Mom's prayers, was Irma bringing me hot coffee at break time. Boy! Did that hit the spot with the snow flying and me shucking corn with my old hat pulled down to keep the blowing snow out of my face and collar. But Ed had a good heart, too. Occasionally, he would remember to bring me a new pair of leather gloves every few days to replace my old ones, which had worn full of holes, when he returned from the domino game, which was a regular thing played on one of the counters at the Petross Store in Claunch about seven miles to the southeast.

The winter weather had decided to get really nasty, and became really unbearable, and I began to wonder whether I would survive it. I remember so well that one day in January, 1942, I was chilled to the point of hypothermia and my hands were almost frozen. The feeling had already left them, and I was trying to rub them together and hold them under my armpits to keep them from freezing. Work had already become impossible, but I dared not to quit for fear of getting fired. Then, what would I do? Where would I go? What would I eat? Where would I sleep? At least, here I had the barn to keep the snow off me and gunny sacks to keep me warm. There was no fear of snakes in the dead of winter either. But, I was almost ready to just give up and die. That would have been easy because I had always heard that when you are cold, all one has to do is go to sleep and death is certain and painless.

One thing that I was not aware of until later is that Evie and Irma were just as concerned as I about my predicament. They were beside themselves, and told me later that they wanted me to move into the house during the cold winter weather, but were afraid to bring up the subject to Ed. But Evie came to me out there shucking corn and freezing and invited me into the house one afternoon while Ed was away playing dominos. YES!! I was ready! I could hardly walk with my frozen feet, but I managed to follow her to the house, some hundred yards, I would guess. The women folks had hot coffee, hot beans and biscuits, and a hot fire in the wood stove. They even had a dry pair of Ed's socks ready and a pair of his shoes and one of his dry jackets. For the first time in a long time, I felt cared for. I felt that someone really cared. The house felt so hot and comfortable when I walked into it, but it seemed to take forever for me to warm up to the point where I felt warm. I think that was the hardest winter I have ever experienced in my entire life! But things were about to take a turn for the better.

When Ed was apprised of my situation in more detail by Evie, he came to me and wanted to know more about my feelings about the situation. Of course, I shared all my feelings with him, even that I didn't mind staying outside, but the extreme cold was a little more than I was equipped to bear. So he asked me to stay in the house with the family and they would arrange somehow room for me a cot of some kind. I could hardly believe my ears, for I really would be very open to anything that would keep me from the extremely frigid nights in the barn, alone and cold. Actually, looking back, it was a miracle I never contracted pneumonia that winter!

A makeshift partition was installed in Irma's bedroom dividing it into two rooms. The larger was hers, and the smaller room was my space into which an old cot was set up for me to put an old single mattress on and some old quilts Evie came up with which were left over from their days on an Oklahoma farm in the years past. But it was light years better than the nothingness I had in the barn. So as it turned out, I had my own little space for a cot, Irma had her bedroom, and Ed and Evie had their privacy in the living room. I was a "kid with a new toy" so to speak. I shall never forget how cozy and warm was my first night there. The storm raged outside, and icicles hung to the ground, but I was as snug as a bug in a rug there on my very own bed in the house. The days and nights passed and spring came. Work continued, but it was a different type of work; spring plowing and all the other chores coupled with getting the new crops into the ground and the fences mended and the machinery readied for the summer season.

CHAPTER 12

* * *

WHAT A WORLD OUT THERE!

T he time came for me to leave the nest, so to speak, and explore
the world. I had heard this term many times during my years
of growing up in central New Mexico, but, then, I had never
been that far from home either. To me, I suppose, this meant going to
Albuquerque or Santa Fe, the state capital. Now *there* was a place to see,
I figured. I had remembered going there ever since Dad took me with
him to one of his barber's conventions there in 1928, the year we had
moved to Albuquerque from the farm. He had worked at that classy
barber shop on Central Avenue called the Sunshine Barber Shoppe,
the best I remember. In Dad's mind, it was the ultimate barber shop
and the owner became Dad's best friend. As the year progressed, Dad's
work became a very important part of his life, and he became second in
command, so-to-speak. He was promoted to *second chair* which put him
in line to participate in various managerial tasks. One of these was to
attend the state barber convention in Santa Fe. I was four, and, therefore,
have no memory of how long the convention lasted, nor just where in
Santa Fe it took place. But one place impressed itself into my memory
indelibly, the New Mexico State Penitentiary, one of the sight-seeing
highlights of the trip.

Dad owned a 1923 Durant sedan back then, and he was very proud
of it. He took every advantage of the times he had off work to take the
family on drives around the nearby area on "outings." So when it came
time to go to Santa Fe to the convention, he drove there in his Durant.
I remember he took me along, just the two of us. I recall the trip quite

well, considering my age, well enough to recall a car on fire alongside the road on the way to Santa Fe. It was just north of Albuquerque a few miles. The site can still be seen today, as I have seen it each of the many times I have traveled that way during my years. The old road, highway 85, was a narrow graveled road which was cut through the hills and were quite infamous for their ability to cause the car's radiator to overheat. Anyway, on the north slope of one of these "cuts," there was this car beside the road on fire. We stopped and looked at it and Dad offered his help, then we were on our way again.

While at the convention during one of Dad's time-off days, Dad took me on a guided tour of the state prison. I will always remember those huge walls with guard houses on their tops at the corners, and the guards walking along the tops of the walls with their big guns. We were inside the walls and the cells all faced the central courtyard where other small buildings were located. I remember there were men prisoners in the bottom cells and women prisoners in the upper rows of cells. There were iron bars on the fronts of all the cells and the prisoners were inside the cells all yelling at us and at each other, especially between the men and the women prisoners. I didn't understand all this and told Dad I wanted to go home. He understood my concern and fright, although I always figured he wasn't quite finished with the prison tour, but we left.

I figured that I could move to Santa Fe and look for work. It had always been a beautiful town which I had a yearning to return to, but had never had the chance. Then there was Albuquerque. Yes, I could move there, also. Albuquerque was a larger city and had much more in the way of excitement and jobs. But perhaps someday I would get to see both places again. I also realized that someday with good luck, I would be traveling much farther from home and be able to see the things I had only read about thus far. Time alone would tell.

However, work on the farm continued the same as usual. As time passed, though, I had this opportunity to change jobs and work for Mr. Draper who had a farm some nine miles to the southeast of where I was at work for Ed. The work was the same but the method of pay was different in that I was to receive fifteen dollars per month and a fourth of the crop at harvest time. This appealed to me because I could envision a huge crop and a lot of money coming my way in the fall. So I accepted the job and moved my things to Mr. Draper's farm. Things, again, were really looking up, I thought.

This was an improvement in living arrangements, to say the least. I had my own room and bed and lived in the big house with the family. It was a large house with four bedrooms. Mr. and Mrs. Draper had their own bedroom, their oldest daughter and her husband and baby had their own bedroom, their youngest daughter and her husband had their own bedroom...AND I had my own bedroom! This was a step in the right direction, I thought, and things went very well. Here, horses were used to plow with, and a new Farmall F-14 tractor was used as well. There was no problem because I was very familiar with all these things and with the crops being raised. So I looked forward to the year, and things went fine for most of the summer. But this was to change!

Near the end of the summer, I was notified that one of the son-in-laws was to move back to the farm and take over the job I was doing. Upon being told this, I inquired about MY future and was told that I was to take the son-in-law's job at the Iceburg Gas Station in Albuquerque. This upset me no end, but there was nothing to be done about it except to accept it and go on with my life. Other jobs were scarce, and I realized it. So, on the given date, my things were loaded into Mr. Draper's '34 Chevy pickup and (I drove, Mr. Draper couldn't drive) we moved me to Albuquerque. I was dumped off at my parents' home and Mr. Draper and his son-in-law returned to Claunch. As a result of all this, I was very hurt and disappointed with people in general, as I explained it all to Mom and Dad, and how I was cheated out of my fourth of the crop. Now, I would have to start from scratch, broke, and much wiser, and make new friends, and begin a new job in this new world...the city.

Since I had no car, I was relegated to riding my brother, Don's, bicycle to work. Now this doesn't sound so bad until one realizes that the trip to the Iceberg Gas Station was quite far. It was four miles across the river, then from that point in the center of town, 120 blocks more on East Central Avenue uphill with some increase of 1500 feet in elevation to the work site, at an hour's strenuous riding. The work shift was from seven PM until seven AM, seven days a week, and I was to be paid two dollars per day and to have no days off and no benefits.

This was a sad turn of events for me and I was stuck with a situation I could not tolerate, but I had no choice but to stick it out. But, then, when would I get a chance to look around for another job? However, this situation sort of worked itself out for the better after a few weeks, at least I thought it had.

Don was working at another gas station on the west side of town and only about three and a half miles from where I was living. A man had quit there which left an opening, and Don recommended me for the job. I was offered the job, and a great feeling of relief passed through my being. Work conditions were to be the same and the pay was to be the same, but, at least, I wouldn't have so far to ride to work. Then, too, this was a fairly new station and everything was freshly painted and the equipment was all new. I could see that this was going to be a fine place to work because never in my life had I ever had all new things at my disposal to do my work. I had no trouble accepting the new job.

I, as on the previous job, worked the night shift from seven to seven, seven days a week. However, I found that I could go to bed about noon and have all morning to myself to take care of personal chores and running around. This worked out fine because I was not so tired from riding so far to work, and it was all level streets to ride upon. The job went well and the routine became habitual and I was pleased with the people I with whom I came in contact. They became good friends in rather short order. The owner of the station, Mr. Johnson (not his real name), owned several other stations all of which he claimed to have the lowest priced gasoline in the state. I can't vouch for that fact, but I do recollect the prices were quite low compared to other stations. The new station where I had hired on was located directly across the street from another gas station and a half-block on west. This station was also owned by Mr. Johnson, but happened to be his old original station where he had his residence in the rear part of the building. I mention this for a reason.

One night late, perhaps about 4:00 A.M., business had slowed to nothing, and I was left sitting waiting for a customer to drive up for service. Quite some time elapsed and I happened to dose my eyes for a moment or two, then with a start, I awakened to find Mr. Johnson standing there looking at me. How embarrassing! I jumped and quickly apologized and went about the chores at hand of cleaning the floors and rest rooms. "Never mind," he said, "You are fired. While you were asleep someone stole a two-gallon can of motor oil from the shelf outside, and I found it missing. Go by the house when you get off at seven and pick up your pay." He walked off if a huff and crossed the street back to his residence.

At seven that morning, Don and the other fellow on the day shift arrived and I explained what had happened to me. They were quite upset and even feared for their own jobs. However, I went over to Mr. Johnson's residence as he had instructed me to do to pick up my pay prior to going home. But when I arrived at his place, but as I knocked on his screen door, my eyes were quickly focused on that two-gallon can of motor oil sitting in the center of his living room floor. I knocked a couple of times before he finally came to the door only to place himself between the can of oil and me to block my view of the can. I was mad! I could hardly speak, I was so mad! I immediately saw what he had done and told him so. He said nothing, but just opened the screen door slightly and handed me my money.

The story, however, does not end there!

To explain, I need to back up a bit to recall that during the war (WW 2), most important items were rationed because the materials were needed in the war effort. This included automobile tires among other things. The government allowed all persons only five tires for their car, and all tires over five had to be turned in to the nearest service station which would pay them one cent per pound for them. This amounted to an average of twenty one cents per tire. The service stations were to turn those tires over to the U.S. government Ration Board in their vicinity for reclaiming into military usage. This brings me up to the subject at hand, Mr. Johnson and his stations. Many people turned in their extra tires and received their twenty one cents per tire. But Mr. Johnson, being the person he was, saw a new way to make quite a profit selling these tires to travelers and local people he could trust to keep their mouths shut about the whole thing. So while I was there, I witnessed quite a number of such sales which irked me no end. So on this, the day of my firing and the day I was accused of being a thief, I decided to do my citizen's duty. I did! I got onto my bicycle and pedaled my way downtown to the Ration Board which was located across from Woolworth's. I parked my bike in the stairwell and went upstairs to report what I had seen happen at the gas station. The head official in the office listened to my story and immediately asked me to accompany him in his car to the station so he could see first hand what was going on. I did. I sat in the car as the agent went inside and purchased a couple of those infamous tires and we returned to his office. He thanked me for being a "good citizen," and I got on by bike and left. I went home to my room and went to bed. I knew that later I would need to find another job, but for now I was tired.

Later on, I learned that Mr. Johnson had been prosecuted, and that he had to sell his holdings to pay the penalties imposed by the court. I have always been taught that "what goes around comes around." I know this to be true, for I have seen it happen many times in many ways. But, for my own future, I needed to get serious and look for another job.

I was sipping a cup of coffee at a nearby café contemplating my situation and visiting with the waitress during a lull in her work. It seemed that my mind wasn't concentrating on what it should have been, though... finding a new job. I suppose I was just winding down from the recent experience with Mr. Johnson. I suppose, also, that I was just catching my breath, so-to-speak. I sipped my coffee and wondered what was to be next in my life.

As I sat at the counter on the stool, I observed a rather tall and lanky well-dressed cowboy-type gentleman enter the café and stand for a moment looking for a likely place to sit. He finally decided to sit at the counter at the place next to me. He ordered coffee and a breakfast and spoke in a very friendly and low-pitched voice. "Good mornin', how are ya," he said. "Hi, I guess I'm ok," I answered. We sat silent for quite a while as we were both finishing our coffee.

"You from around here?" "Yeah," I said, "I live with my folks across the river in Armijo." I had no idea who he was, but he was a very likable sort and I liked him right off. We exchanged pleasantries for a while, then he asked, "Could I hire you to take me back home? I don't drive and my boy has just joined the Air Force and left me here with his car." I asked how that happened, because it sounded crazy to me. I didn't understand at all. Then he clarified the situation by adding, "Oh, we live close to Carlsbad and my boy came up to Albuquerque to join the Air Force, but I can't drive his car home. I don't drive." "Oh, I get it now."

He said to me, "My name is White. Jim White. I live in White's City right by Carlsbad. I am the guy that discovered the Carlsbad Caverns, I guess you might've heard of 'em." " Yeah, I've seen 'em, I've been in 'em, on a school trip in '37." "You found 'em?" "Yeah, I did. But can you drive me home?" "Yeah, I will. But I have to tell my folks first so they won't worry about me."

"Fine! I think that's a good idee."

As it turned out, Mr. White and his son had been staying at a nearby tourist court where the son's new '41 Mercury convertible was left parked when he took the city bus to Kirtland Air Force Base when he reported to duty. Mr. White took me over and showed me the car and gave me the keys, and he loaded his suitcases into the car. We drove by Mom and Dad's place and picked up my clothes and razor and comb and headed toward White's City. Instead of taking the main highways, I chose to take the back roads for the 300-mile trip. I was very familiar with every road in that part of New Mexico, and I wanted to show Mr. White where I was raised and introduce him to some of my friends. There seemed to be no set schedule, so we decided to make a leisurely trip out of it. So we did just that.

Our first stop was Ed Bogges's place where I began my work career, as I have described previously. Jim, as I came to call him, and Ed became great friends immediately and both told tales of their pasts, and I listened intently as did Irma and Evie. Several days were spent there, and several trips were made to Claunch to the liquor store to satisfy both Jim and Ed's thirsts. They were both devout story tellers from the past and thouroughly well-experienced drinkers, as well, when the opportunity presented itself, and they proved to be extremely well matched in those arenas. Irma, Evie, and I thoroughly enjoyed the humorous and, occasionally, ridiculous stories that literally brought tears to our eyes.

It was the rainy season which turned all dirt roads into deep quagmires of sticky mud which relegated us all to the living room most of the time. It also gave us all a chance to learn more about Jim White and his stories of just how he came to discover and develop the great cave known and Carlsbad Caverns. I shall relate some of the stories they told in the following paragraphs:

Baby Switch

Ed grew up in the timbered eastern Oklahoma hills where civilization had hardly shown its face during the late '80s. Young folks, as he put it, "Didn't have no way to do much to do to entertain themselves. So boys would get together and figger out sumpthin' to do fer fun. Or just to "raise hell."

"So this one summer'" he continued, "they were a havin' a revival out there at that little church in the woods all by itself, and not too fur frum our place, maybe a mile or two. People would come before dark in their wagons and buggies by the dozens and park them all 'round that church and leave thu' babies asleep there on quilts n' blankets in their buggy or wagon, and go on in the Church and have their revival.

Us boys in our family, there wuz three uv us, got to talkin' and figgered it'd be a hell-uv-a-lot-uv-fun to go out there and switch them babies all around. "Well," he continued, "We took them babies one at a time and put them all in different buggies from where they were s'posed to be and switched them all around. I don't think we left one of them in the right wagon or buggy. 'Course, when all the noise and hollerin' frum the revival wuz over the people started cumin' out to their buggies and wagons, an' bein' dark an' all, they couldn't see much 'bout thu' babies, so they all went on home takin' the kids with'm."

But, Ed went on, "So us boys figger'd we needed to foller one of'm on home and watch thru' thu' winder' when they lit the coal-oil lamp. So we did. They did. That daddy and momma sure 'nuff cum apart when they saw they had thu' wrong kid! Ed always laughed as he told his own stories and this was no exception. Through tears of laughter and laughing, he went on as best he could,"When them folks saw they had the wrong kid all hell broke loose n' they headed straight back to the church." But he went on to tell that not everyone returned to church. Some told the law. Some took their rifles and went looking for whoever did this terrible thing. But the boys, however, figured they better lay low and circled around and went straight home and sneaked into bed without even their folks being any the wiser of what had happened. He said they were visited by the law, but their folks swore the "boys were at home in bed."

"It musta took all of two weeks fer them kids to all git straightened out, but us boys sure kep' our mouths shet fer a long time...'til we moved kleen outa Oklahomie," he told through hillariious laughter.

Crawling Out of Carlsbad Cavern—In The Dark

Jim White was a cowboy in the most real and original sense of the word. Yes, Jim, as everyone knew him, related that he spent his younger years riding the range of a large ranch west of Carlsbad, New Mexico and doing all the various types of work that needed doing. He told of his life there and also told of all the sorrows and happiness and fears and comforts and discomforts one could experience in the unsettled, desolate, cruel, untamed, and hot desert southwest. He told of the rattlesnakes crawling into his bedroll with him at night as he slept where they could share the warmth of his body. He also eluded to the painful experiences which taught him to search his bedroll for scorpions before crawling into it. He described the hot winds of summer blowing the desert sands into his eyes as he searched for lost cattle and orphaned calves among the cholla (pronounced choya) cacti.

He told of those long days which began at daybreak and ended after dark. He spoke of the ever-so-painful loneliness which never ended with the workday, but continued with each sunrise and how his horse was truly his only friend for weeks on end as he rode the hundreds of miles of fence and gullies and ridges, just to repeat it all again. He told of how the earth and God were his only companions with whom he could converse and share his most inner feelings, his love, and his tears and laughter. He told of the huge expanse of desert as his home, his castle, his bedroom, his cathedral, his toilet, his breadbasket of nourishment.

A real cowboy was he, a cowboy whom NO movie ever truly depicted then or now. Jim White!!

Actually, as Jim said to me, he was not out looking for a cave. No, he was just ending one of his days of riding a 30- mile fence line when he pulled up his horse and stopped to observe the sunset, one of hundreds he had witnessed there in the New Mexico desert on the southern expanses of the Guadalupe Mountains, there where one can see forever.

As he sat there on his horse taking in all of God's beautiful handiwork as the sun was sinking low in the west, his attention was suddenly directed to a sunken spot on a nearby hill top where bats were emerging from the earth. Yes! Millions of them flying right out of the ground and disappearing into the distance. In amazement, he dismounted and stood in the midst of one of the greatest sights he had ever witnessed, he told me. Never, he said, did he ever see such an amazing sight, and he said that he told himself that he had to go to that spot immediately and see the place from where the bats had emerged. What kind of a hole in the ground was it that so many bats could live in and emerge so quickly.

He remounted his horse and rode quickly to the place of emergence, which was not so very far away from where he had made the unusual observation, to be confronted with the opening of a large cave. The opening, he related, was so deep that the bottom could not be seen from any vantage point he could find. Of course, he said, that darkness was upon him and he decided to return the next morning early and go into the cave to investigate.

Jim related to me that very early the next morning before daylight, he prepared the items he figured he would need to go down into the entrance and look around to see what he could see. Actually, he said, he was interested in where the bats were coming from, the place they lived down there in the earth.

"I figur'd it had to be a pretty big cave to hold that many bats. "I didn't have no rope long enuf to reach that fer in the cave, he said, "But, I didn't see no bottom 'cause it were dark down there n' there wuz a bend in the openin' that blocked my view." So he decided to use barbed wire from the nearby cattle fence to make a makeshift ladder that he could hang into the cave.

Also, Jim fitted a coal oil (kerosene) can with a rope wick and also carried with him a spare can of coal oil should he need it. He also took several other items he figured he would need such as food and water. So with these items and plans, Jim said he returned to the cave opening and stripped off enough barbed wire from the fence and built the wire ladder of which he fastened one end to a secure rock and lowered the rest of it into the cave entrance. He said that he then climbed down the ladder to its end, which, incidentally didn't reach the bottom of the cave, and managed to follow ledges and rocks and work his way to what he thought was the bottom. His impression of the situation, he iterated, was one of extreme surprise. He said he was totally in disbelief of how big the cave was where those bats lived, the 'Bat Cave," as it was later named.

In the months to follow, he said that he made many trips into the cave and learned there were many caves that led off from the entrance, but one was much larger than the others and was of great interest to him, so he concentrated on it mostly. He told of many experiences he had while exploring this massive complex of underground caves and how he almost thought he was a "goner" on several occasions. One of these, I found very interesting and most frightening, and kept me on the edge of my chair as he told it in his own vernacular.

Jim told of this experience which occurred on one trip, his second, explaining that he had climbed down the wire ladder and made his way to the flat surface below where he proceeded on toward unknown territory. The cave abruptly turned downward very steeply and the floor consisted of huge rocks, some a hundred or more feet high, which had fallen from the ceiling many millennia previously. One of those rocks he later named the "Iceburg" because of its size, and the fact that the bottom two thirds of it cannot be seen because of much debris covering the lower portion of it.. However, Jim related that he was carefully making his way down the slick surfaces of those huge rocks downward into the total darkness of the unknown depths of that huge cave. Suddenly, his torch can slipped from his hands and went tumbling downward into the depths of the unknown. There he was without any light whatsoever. His words to me were something like this as he recalled the experience to me that day.

"...I know'd I was a gonna die in there, in that there dark place if I didn't do somethin' to get outa there. I didn't have no light, so I figgered that I had been goin' down ever since I got into that cave, so I know"d I would have to go "up" if I wuz a gonna get outa there. So I turned 'round and started to crawl up the rocks to find my way back to whur I could see light agin. It wuz about a half a mile, but it seemed like a hunerd miles." Jim also remembered, "...I bet it took me two days to find my way back to the ladder. I crawled and crawled and rested and kept doin' it 'til I got sleepy. I would sleep 'til I would wake up an' I wud start to crawl agin'. I finly' saw a tiny light from the place I come in, n' I know'd I would make it out, then."

He told many stories of his experiences during the exploring of the cave and of him taking others from all over the world into it to show them what he had found. He told of how no one believed him at first, and of how that was the reason he took a few people to go with him in order to prove that it did exist and that he in fact did see what he said he saw. It wasn't many months until enough people came to tour the cave that he began to improve the ladder and started to build trails and use better lights. Later the U.S. government came to him and wanted to make it a national attraction and put him as the superintendent of it. The rest is history and appears in several books written by several authors including Jim White himself. I have his book of the Carlsbad Caverns and was fortunate to become great friends with both Jim and his Wife and their daughter. I also was fortunate to be invited to stay with them in their home in White's City after driving Jim back from that Albuquerque trip in 1941. I am also proud to have been their guest twice into the caverns and to participate at their concession there in the Large Room in the Lunch Pavilion near the elevators. A truly wonderful family whom I truly enjoyed and miss very much since their passing. The Carlsbad Caverns in New Mexico have since become one of the most famous caverns and natural attractions on earth, and is listed by most as one of the seven original "wonders of the world."

That brief encounter with the White family, which turned out to be one of the most enjoyable three weeks I can remember off hand, had to come to an end, as all things do, and I again faced the reality of unemployment.

I did manage to secure several short-term jobs in order to exist, but I never was able to locate the position where I felt comfortable with either the work itself or the security of my future. I worked as a grocery delivery person, a freight handler and delivery person, and as a telephone central office equipment installer for the Rocky Mountain Bell Telephone Company in Albuquerque. I think the later was the most promising position I had been able to secure up to that point in my life. However, about six months after I had started work there, the labor union decided to strike. I was informed by the union steward that I had to go along with the strike or else I wouldn't be allowed to participate in any benefits the union would obtain as a result of the strike. Well, as you can imagine, I had no reserve bank account, nor was I in any condition to weather out a 6-month-long strike without pay. So I did what I had to do. I told the steward where he could stick the union and the job if that was his attitude. So I began another fruitless hunt for a good job, one with a future. Job openings were almost unheard of, and I was faced with living with my parents there in Albuquerque until I could find something.

Being the sensitive person that I was, and am, I wouldn't allow myself to sponge off my parents any longer, so I, again, turned to the farm life at Claunch where I, at least, knew people. Ed put me to work right away, again, and I assumed the role of supervisor of the field crew cleaning weeds from the crop with hoes. Then, came the harvest crew. Then came winter again, and the corn picking by hand and the shucking which followed. Big difference this time around: I had a place inside to stay out of the weather at night.

Then came early December, 1942.

Irma went to the rural mail box located on the road in front of the house, and retrieved the mail from within it. She stood for a moment staring at a letter she had gotten from the mail box. Then, she quickly turned and ran back to the house yelling, "Forrest! Forrest, you got a letter from the draft board."

I didn't believe my ears. I knew there was a war going on. I knew I had registered for service as was the requirement for all males over 18. But I had, somehow, forgotten the reality of it all, I suppose, and never realized that I and a lot of other boys would actually be called for service. But here it was!

"Forrest, did you hear what I said?"

Yes, I had heard her, alright! I didn't want to believe it, though. She handed me the letter. I opened it.

"GREETINGS!"

"You are hereby ordered to report to ..."

Signed, "Franklin D. Roosevelt, President of the United States."

CHAPTER 13

* * *

"HUT TWO THREE FOUR ... HUT ... HUT..."

The war had been going on for about two years when I received my formal draft notice to report for induction into the United States Army, even though I had been required to register for military service just after the declaration of war. There were several theoretical reasons the draft board waited those two years to induct me, but there was only one real reason. This was that I was a farm hand and farming was considered a "war effort" and people working therein were exempted from the draft. Another reason was that I was married. So to completely understand this situation, I will need to go back a couple of years to when I was in high school.

As explained earlier, I had spent a bit over four years working on farms other than Dad's. One of them was the Lavelle farm which was managed by Ed Bogges. Ed's youngest daughter, Irma, and I had known each other since we were in elementary school and had always been very good friends. In fact, we had always been great friends and found ourselves talking often and seemed to have a lot of things in common and seemed to naturally gravitate toward each other, although our technical interests were totally opposite. She was anything but technical. I, on the other hand, have always been highly technical, but we did like to just sit and look at each other, and, then, too, we did have much in common such as baseball and other sports, country music and country dances. I couldn't dance, so I played the guitar to accompany

Bill Galloway's fiddle on Saturday nights. She was a good dancer, and enjoyed dancing with everyone at those dances, since she knew all of them. Shucks, as they would say, everybody knew everybody.

We often just hung around the school library and the pitcher pump at the cistern and talk. (The school's drinking water supply comprised two deep cisterns, equipped with pitcher pumps, located on the north side of the school building.) The rest of the kids often teased us and accused us of "going together" and being sweethearts. Of course, this was not true at all, at that time, that is. But I'll admit that we did hold hands whenever we could get out of eye-shot of everyone else, she being just as eager as I.

With that background, it becomes easier to understand that when I moved into the Bogges household during that terribly cold winter, It placed Irma and me in close proximity to each other, much closer than before. We did spend much time on weekends playing Chinese checkers and poker and other card games, and did become much closer and did, in fact, start "going together." However, we were accompanied by Evie, Irma's mother, everywhere we went. No Sir, Evie couldn't release Irma from her apron strings, even at age 18. But even with that handicap, we did manage to become engaged to be married on June 15th, 1941.

The wedding was to be a simple one to take place in front of Ed's and Evie's house on a bright sunny day. The presiding official was to be Bill Galloway, Justice-of-the-Peace and neighbor and the fiddler with whom I played at the country dances, some of them at this very house on many Saturday nights.

Irma was to wear a blue dress that she herself had made for the occasion, and I was to wear my cheap black suit which I had managed to get Dad to buy for me when I had performed in a high school play a couple of years previous. To my recollection, I believe the suit cost the huge sum of eleven dollars and was ordered from Montgomery Ward in Denver. It never did really, what you would call, fit, but it served the purpose(s) in its own baggy way. But there comes to mind a comical and not-so-unique- for-those-times story which I shall share at this point.

During my tenure at Tularosa High School, Irma and I would write constantly to each other, secretly, I might add, because her folks prohibited her from going with boys for fear they would destroy her innocence. Well, we did write clandestinely, and her innocence never suffered in the least. As for the "blue wedding dress she made, it was blue because that's all the material she had and couldn't afford to purchase new material of the customary white color that would advertise her virginity. Her mother, Evie, made the remark, "Who cares, I think blue is prettier than white anyway."

The story of the rings is interesting as well.

While goofing off one day after school, I happened upon a used wedding and engagement ring set at this same second hand store where I had traded my beautiful new violin for that case-less guitar? I noticed the set had a price tag of eleven dollars. I went to the owner and asked whether he would take payments. "Sure!" "Are you going to get married or something, or is this for a friend of yours?" He knew I was only sixteen, almost seventeen. Although I looked at myself as a grown man, he, being of much more maturity than I, was also very much wiser and knew I was much too young for such a purchase.

"Oh, no," I responded. "It's ME that needs it. I am the one getting married." "U Huh," he eventually replied, looking over his small round glasses.

I made the purchase and managed to pay for it a dollar or so at a time, and eventually was permitted to take it home to Mrs. Hagee's house and hide it securely, figuring that someday Irma and I would certainly use it. Weeks passed many SWAK letters were exchanged, and the relationship heated to the point of me asking that all-important question in one of the letters. Although I asked the question, it hardly was necessary because we both had, for months, talked all around the subject and already "knew" we were going to get married one day. So the built-in assumption became reality with the "question" and I sent her the engagement ring in a subsequent letter.

The other part of the story takes place several months later and is about the trip to buy the marriage license at the court house in Estancia, New Mexico. I begins this way:

Ed and his other helper, Leonard Goad, were working in one of the fields located some three miles from the house, but Leonard had left his car, a 1929 Oldsmobile 4-door sedan parked at Ed's house and had driven Ed's '35 Chevy sedan to work instead, since it was in much better mechanical condition. Irma, myself, and Evie were alone at the house trying to figure a way to get to Estancia to get the license. You see, Evie actually was on our side in planning the marriage and even helped keep things from Ed, If Ed had known even half of the things happening, we would have raised "holy Ned," as she put it. So to keep things running halfway smoothly, we just let him learn much later.

Then I had a beautiful thought. Take Leonard's car. We could be back before they got in from work (about dark). So the three of us piled into Leonard's Olds sedan and headed for Gran Quivera. We stopped there to get some gas for the car "on credit," because it was that we didn't have any money. Mrs. Turner, the owner's wife of the store said to us, "Well you probably got here just in time."

She went to the door and looked out to see whether Jones (her husband) was about ready to leave, then told us, "Jones is gittin' ready to go to Mountainair to get some stuff fer the store, and you all kin ride in the back uf th' truck (a brand-new 1- 1/2-ton Chevy truck) up there. He would just take you on over t' Estanchy to git the license n' back."

"OK," Evie said, and we climbed up into the stake-side bed of the new Chevy truck, and off we went, holding onto the sides as we flew over the gravel highway those fifty miles to the court house to get the ever-so important- marriage license.

Of course we all had been to Estancia many times over the years for one reason or another and all knew the small town very well. Jones drove right up to the court house and we all climbed down and went into the court house and into the county clerk's office. From there, it was all new to me. We answered the questions, Irma told her true age, Evie vouched for her, I lied about my age, the clerk looked at me rather strangely, then signed and sealed the license.

"Twenty five cents, please, sir."

Had I been wearing false teeth, I would have dropped them on the spot! Why, I hadn't even given a thought of paying any money for a license. I guess I figured it would be free. Fact is, I guess I hadn't even thought about it at all, to be truthful.

"Twenty five cents?"

"Yes, Sir."

I stuck my hand in my pocket, but I knew full well there was nothing at all in it, much less money. All in the world I carried in my pocket was a few kitchen matches to light my roll-your-own Dukes Mixture cigarettes. I looked at Irma, then at Evie. "Let me see if I have any money."

After rummaging through her fifty-year-old purse and fingering through many year's-worth of "goodies," she exclaimed, "Here's a quarter! It was way down in the bottom of my purse." She handed it to the clerk, and I breathed a sigh of great relief, and vowed to myself quietly to NEVER get into this kind of situation ever again. I would always KNOW ahead of time that I could arrange payment and never make an ass of myself again, EVER.

Back on the truck and headed homeward, I leaned over and whispered into Evie's ear, "Thank You." She gave me a little kiss with her snuff-stained lips on the cheek and smiled. We were always the best of friends, Evie and I.

The trip back from Estancia was, for the most part uneventful, except for the necessary stops in Mountainair to pick up supplies for Jones' general store. The wind blew fiercely into our faces as the truck sped homeward, so much so that we handed the new marriage license up front for them to put it into the glove compartment to prevent the wind from blowing it right out of our hands there in the back of the moving truck.

"Thanks a million, Jones, fer th' ride" I yelled at Jones as I hurriedly went to the car to take it back home for Leonard to have when he would come in from the fields. "Don't mention it," he replied as he began unloading the truck.

The trip was a great success and we arrived back at Ed's house without fanfare and much before he came in from the fields. No one was the wiser!

The next few days were kind of hectic and busy for the women folks, I suppose, but life for us men went on as usual, field work and the like. But the time arrived and it was June 15th. I realized that word gets around in a small rural community, but I never thought so many people lived in those parts. People from all over started arriving in all sorts of vehicles, BUT they were ALL dressed up in their very best "bib-and-tucker." And I knew ALL of them. They had come from as far away as twenty miles or more. They brought gifts and were all aglow and covered with broad smiles as Irma and I repeated our vows and said our *I do* to each other. Then the party began and it was a day to remember, that day out there in the country in front of the folks' house on that bright sunny day in June. But the fun times couldn't last. Tomorrow was work day again, and work we had to. The crops needed tending in order to get them laid by for summer. A "honeymoon" was for the "rich." It was for those in story books, and for those who didn't have to work so hard to survive. But, as we dreamed our dreams, we planned to also be well off some day, then we, too could have a honeymoon, YES we looked forward to THAT, someday!

But in the recesses of our minds, we both knew that somewhere Uncle Sam was lurking and waiting his turn to change all our plans. Change them he did!

On January 7, 1943, I was to report for duty at Fort Bliss, Texas. But, first, I had to report to the state capital, Santa Fe, and meet with the other hundreds of draftees for our physical examinations, then a week later, I had to travel to Socorro, the county seat, to catch the army troupe train and travel to El Paso, Texas where we boarded army trucks for the trip to Fort Bliss. It was an interesting trip because all windows had the blinds drawn and we were instructed to not look out of them to see where we were going. It was all "classified" they said, and that we new recruits would be quickly taught about such matters. Meanwhile, we were told to forget what we see and discuss NOTHING with anyone at any time, EVER!

Upon arrival at the U.S. Army Induction Center on the Army Base at Fort Bliss, we were marched directly from those army trucks to a parade ground and lined up and sorted out into alphabetical order by "role call," a term we were to hear several times each day for the duration of our time spent in the army. It seems that after every function, we had to line up as demanded by the Sergeant's very loud and totally audible whistle blast. Also we were taught very early on that we were to "fall in" in alphabetical order for everything, including payday and also to line up at the mess hall door prior to being allowed to "quietly" and "orderly" enter the mess hall where we had to stand behind the assigned bench at the 10-man table where we were to sit to partake of our *wonderful and very nutritious meal* that had been prepared by the "world's best" cooks. AND who were we to question this? If we had, it meant a weekend of "KP" duty. We soon learned the exact meaning of that two-letter abbreviation. "**Kitchen Police.**"

As days passed, we were alphabetically lined up to receive our many shots, attend many lectures pertaining to sexually-transmitted diseases and military discipline and just how to wear the highly respected uniform of the United States Army. Other pertinent information was being transfused into our tender young brains by various means including much instruction and by the complex technique of group marching. We also found ourselves being moved to a new training facility.

Again, the travel was by army truck to the railway yards in El Paso where our "troupe train" was waiting our arrival. Only this time, it was a Pullman train with "blinds drawn.". The time was night and we all settled into our assigned compartments. We waited for movement of the train, but gave that up after a few hours and decided that the army would do as they wanted and would not share any plans with the likes of us lowly recruits. But as we climbed into our bunks, the train slowly began to maneuver its way out of the yards, and with all the direction changing, we soon lost our bearings and had absolutely no idea which direction we were headed once we got under way. The lonesome cry of the steam locomotive's whistle gave no clue except that there were numerous road crossings. Even those became almost non-existent as we traveled into the dark night. I must confess, however, that I sneaked a look out my window when the engineer broke the silence of the night with a series of whistles I happened to recognize as a "Yard Limits" signal. Yep! We were entering the yards of a large town. I saw desert vegetation. I saw palm trees. I recognized Phoenix. We were headed WEST!

The train did not stop. It continued at a good clip, and again entered the desert and the whistle again relaxed as if readying itself for the next round of signals somewhere down the line. I tried to sleep, but somehow my thoughts wandered to the folks at home. I thought of my mother, my mother who worried a lot about me in the catacombs of her mind because Dad would usually make negative comments to her regarding such concern about her children's wellbeing. He figured us kids should figure out our own solutions for our own problems and situations. But Mom was a good mom and cried for our pains and hurts and our unhappy situations; my being inducted into the army was hard for to come to grips with and she quietly shed many tears of love for me during those trying times.

The train pulled into a military base and slowly came to a stop. Our "proctors" hurried us off the train and had us "fall in" beside our own train cars for roll call. Again, we were loaded onto army trucks which were waiting beside the tracks in precisely the correct spots. After a few minutes travel the trucks pulled up near the empty barracks which we were to occupy to form the new 548th Antiaircraft Artillery Battalion. My group was to be known as Battery "B." My new address was to be: BtryB548thAAAbn United States Army, Serial Number 38350149.

The rain came down and the heavy fog persisted. This was grossly different climate from that we had just left at Fort Bliss, near El Paso. This was, indeed, our introduction to a new world: The Army and Camp Haan, California! It was very early in the morning, before daylight, and we were given time to settle in and hang our newly issued uniforms and other items and fall out for calisthenics, roll call, AND breakfast. And so was my introduction into a situation over which I had absolutely NO control, nor from which I had no escape. We were now a small part of the 70,000 soldiers being trained at this new Army base situated just across the highway from March Air Base (the P-38 Lightning and the B-24 Liberator) which served the Pacific Theater of Army Operations. We, as the song goes, "were in the army now, Mr. Jones."

We ALL knew about the 15-hour KP days which began at 0300 and ended at 2100, and if we dared a second negative remark, we also knew that KP could go on forever, and ever, and ever, AMEN!! Believe me, it could!! We were also aware that if this KP thing should happen to us, we would miss out on all those 10-mile hikes, those 25-mile hikes, and those 50-mile overnighters. OH!! I forgot to mention those obstacle courses and those gunnery sessions and rifle exercises on our bellies under live machine gunfire, *and* those practice trips through the war-gas chambers filled with real gas such as chloropicrin gas, mustard gas, and the like. I shouldn't forget "tear Gas" either, it was so much fun, especially exhausting it from our gas masks which had to be put on AFTER we entered the war-gas chamber! Yes, as the sergeant explained on so many training occasions, "You bastards be damn sure to leave your gas masks OFF until you get inside. When you get in there, you are still holding your breath as you gently and slowly place the mask over your face and pull the strap over the top of your head. Then lift one side of your mask with one finger and EXHALE HARD as you remove your finger. That's how you do it and I don't want ANY ......-ups! Do you understand me??" We very quickly learned the hard way that if one were to breathe the least bit of that gas into their lungs, immediate vomiting into the gas mask would be the most unhappy result. Oh, yes, need I mention that if this did happen, one could not possibly remove the mask to clean it out until *after* they exited the chamber some minutes later. The army has its own way of teaching lessons the hard way, lessons never to be forgotten, they were!

NO! I wouldn't dare have messed up deliberately to get on KP so that I would miss out on all those *wonderful* events, NO WAY!!

PART TWO

*From the Tranquility of That
New Mexico Farm Country,
I was catapulted into the Hustle and Bustle,
Discipline of the United States Army, and the
Many Sides of*

World War II

*....Immorality, and Chaos; the Perpetrator of International Strife
Felt "Round the World;"
The Beginning of the End of Family Unity and
Respect.*

*"...it's The Uniform You Salute!"
Said he, the*

FIRST SERGEANT

CHAPTER 14
* * *
HERE I AM, LORD

But, had I had total say in my future planning, the army would have been way down the list, perhaps clear off the bottom. But since one has to face reality most of the time during their lifespan, I realized that there was no way in heck I could erase any of this new stuff that was happening to me. Hate it as I did and thinking that good old farm life would be really a lot better even with all those hardships and cold nights, little did I realize that there were more hardships and even colder nights awaiting my presence. Now don't get me wrong. There were those who ate it up. Yeah! They DID! Big time! Just to get away from Mom and Dad and not have to obey those "rules" and account for their every act, most of which would have had doubtful acceptability at home. Same with the girlfriends back home. WOW, if only they could have been proverbial flies on the wall.

As for my private life in the army, which was very miniscule, so to speak, I was not only too bashful and shy for such shenanigans, but Mom had taught me well and had me knowing that God himself followed me everywhere I went and no way could I even think of "hiding" from Him; that He sees everything I do and hears everything I think or say. So that in itself put the fear into my very bones to even try to do anything that I was certain to have to explain and have held against me on judgment day. So routine behavior was IT! Arise at five AM six days a week, take care of those latrine duties, dress, stand roll call, and go get our very nourishing and delicious breakfast of shit on a shingle (SOS), gray coffee (which had been boiled in a huge iron pot which makes perfectly good coffee turn to a nasty gray substance no self-respecting hog would admit having in its swill). Then we had to put our bunks in order and left them inspection-ready. Then off to classes and other work which our leaders had so very carefully and deliberately planned to beautify our day.

Our families were, of course, concerned for us being in the services and for our welfare and placed a star in their windows to indicate they had a son in service for our country. My parents were no different.

My father, Oscar, (WW1 Veteran), Deceased; My Sister, Jewel, My Mother, Elda (also deceased).

We all had to undergo gunnery training on every type of gun and cannon and rocket that we would be living with forever. Since we were the 548th Antiaircraft Artillery battalion, our weapons to master were the mobile 40-mm automatic antiaircraft machine gun which fired a 40-mm (about 1 1/2 inches) projectile that was loaded with explosive and could knock down an aircraft about 3000 feet in the air. Also there were smaller guns such as the 50-caliber, water-cooled antiaircraft machine gun that would fire about a thousand rounds per minute, and then, the 50-caliber air-cooled machine gun, just as fast but a bit more portable. Then there was the 45-caliber Thomson submachine gun, the M1 Carbine rifle, the M1 Garand rifle, and a host of smaller devices such as grenades and so forth.

Not only did we have to learn to become expert at firing and transporting the weapons, their safety, and how to maintain them (cleaning, lubricating, polishing parts and the like), we had to learn how to overhaul and repair them under battlefield environmental conditions. The smaller weapons disassembly and reassembly had to be memorized so that we could accomplish this in the darkness of night by feel....with NO mistakes.

Of course, those of us who were team leaders had to be assigned trucks, weapons carriers and jeeps and had to attend a very lengthy driver's school and be tested (500 questions plus driver's test in the vehicles) and army-licensed to drive all them. My license included everything except aircraft, motorcycles, and tanks. I also was sent to radio school and later became section leader of the radio/telephone section of Battery B. This training included so many methods and secrets of laying portable telephone lines both through all of the dozens of front line gun positions and back to the commanders' positions and portable switchboards. We were also taught to sabotage the enemies" phone lines so many ways to prevent them from having communications capabilities. This was not a singular action, but they were sabotaging our lines as well. They, the enemy, would go along our lines, which were twisted pair wires laid along the ground. They would take straight pins (the ones used for sewing) and stick them through the twisted pair thus shorting the line. They would do this at night about every few yards and clip the ends of the pins off flush with the outside of the pair. So we did the same to them. We were taught to locate the short and remove the pin as soon as we could in order to restore phone service. Radio communications was by portable radios installed in all vehicles and at all command locations and gun positions. So it was my job to also keep those radios in working order and replaced if too damaged. Also, we in our radio section had a large radio transmitter and receiver which functioned as the Battery Commander's communication capability over longer distances to other batteries and battalions. I of course kept that system going as well. Each Battery had identical equipment and used different call letters to identify their unit.

Then training wound down and we were sent to the staging area to wait to be deployed overseas; but, then, a very interesting and, perhaps shocking, thing occurred. I shall explain.

Private Forrest Newitt Easley.

CHAPTER 15

* * *

GUINEA PIG???

I will say that the army sometimes has very interesting experiences to be had. Now with that said, I shall just lightly mention that after we had been given all that training and after we had eaten of the sands of the greater Mojave Desert as it was sprinkled onto our C-rations by the summer's winds, and after we had soaked up all that wonderful hot desert July sunshine near Bad Water, Death Valley, (right at 135 degrees F. as we measured it on those days as we stood watch for Japanese zeros), our outfit finally returned to our original army base staging area at Camp Haan, California to await deployment overseas. (Now, how's that for a nice long sentence? :)

NOTE: I suppose it is proper at this point to explain the comment above which refers to our standing watch for Japanese Zero aircraft in the middle of Death Valley. Kind of odd, don't you think, that a fine group of American soldiers with assumed good sense would go the center of Death Valley, to the lowest and hottest part of it no less, to look for Japanese airplanes flying overhead to bomb our country? Yeah, right! I agree it really does! However, I am here to tell you that is exactly what we were doing out there. We were! Yeah, in *July* of all seasons. And you won't believe it, but that sounds like we were nuts! But, consider the month, consider the temperature, and consider that, also, the sky was without any trace of a cloud and the sun beamed down upon us like a huge blowtorch. Yes, we wore our overcoats to keep from utterly burning up. Yeah, you catch on fast, we also wore our helmet liners and steel helmets to protect our heads as well. In fact it was so blamed hot that the 4 x 4 truck we were driving into that desert refused to quit running when the driver turned off the ignition key. It just kept on *dieselling*...had to choke it to kill it.

Never in my life shall I ever forget those few days that we sat on that hilltop there in that desert sun looking through binoculars for those small Jap fighter plans which also carried bombs.

It is also fitting to let you in on a small military secret (as it was back then).

One evening just after we had arrived back to the staging area and we all had turned in just after the taps bugle was played at 2100, the air raid siren started to sound. Now all well trained soldiers upon hearing an air raid siren know not to dilly-dally but to get into their boots, gas mask, helmet, and grab their weapon and disperse as they were (naked) over a wide area so as to guard against being all killed, but, instead, to keep the casualties to a minimum. So here we were: one thousand naked guys with their guns, boots, gas masks, and helmets laying on their bellies on that brush covered hillside watching those several Jap Zeros flying high overhead as our powerful searchlights followed them inland. As the larger guns fired at those high-flying planes, we watched in horror there below. (It is not known just how many latrines might have....been....utilized....during....those....several....frightening.... moments, but I would hazard a guess that dry hillside became much damper that night.

The planes circled around and eventually flew back out to sea without any indication of invasive activity.

So with that being explained, here we were back to barracks in which to live, real food in the mess hall, and real latrines to shave, shower,, and pee in, and things seemed fairly good again. I could again eat without having sand mixed into the scrambled eggs. However, very soon after our arrival, the situation was to drastically change. I was called to report to the dispensary medics. From there I was transported to the front entrance of the West Coast Army Regional Hospital at Camp Haan and was led to the log-in desk (different terminology than in "civilian" hospitals. No monkey business here. No large bunches of female "nurses" to hand you a form to fill out telling your entire family history, and make one sit for hours waiting to see the doctor. Nope! Just guy nurses who got straight to the point.

"Private Easley?" "Yes sir." "Go down that hallway to room S-5 and report to Doctor Galloway (not his real name), he's expecting you."

After knocking, saluting, and standing at attention, Doctor Galloway, Captain, US Army, asked me to be seated.

I was told that there was some indication from my unit dispensary that there was a urinary problem and that they were to try a series of experimental cystotomy procedures on me.

I was assigned a bed in that 36-bed S-5 ward where I was to spend the next several weeks to undergo five experimental surgical procedures. Of course, there were those 3-inch-long needles they used to inject novocaine into my spine each time. If ever I could learn to hate anything, I believe it was during these months. The excruciating pain one cannot possibly imagine until they would have walked in the shoes I did at that time. Each time a procedure was performed, every two or three weeks, five spinal shots were given using that same size needle and pain killer. I was told by the male nurse that these five shots each time by far exceeded any spinals given for child birth or regular surgery in the lower body. He was right because when I had hip surgery later on, those spinal shots were comparatively mild to those there in S-5. But, I suppose it was all for a good purpose. I was told that the information gained from those procedures tried would be passed along to medical schools and civilian medical institutions. It seems I wasn't the only soldier being experimented upon. All I do know for sure is that even at the time of this writing, certain side effects of that "surgery" still persists and cause a certain amount of discomfort in my kidneys and ureters, and bladder. Also urination has been somewhat unpredictable and embarrassing and difficult.

It was a very welcome day when I was released back to my outfit. The time spent in that hospital had actually served also to accustom me to a different life style, so to speak. Now, I was back to routine classes, KP duty, policing up the area as a group each morning, and continuously maintaining the weapons and other equipment we were assigned to such as radio equipment and vehicles. Of course there were those who insisted on screwing up by being AWOL a few hours getting back from their leave, or by messing up some other way. The usual punishment for those "crimes" was to be assigned to dig a six-by-six. For those of you who weren't in the army, a six-by-six is a hand-dug hole in the hardest of ground that had to be dug six feet square and six feet deep with a pick and shovel. This was not a thing that could be accomplished in an afternoon. Of course the season again was the middle of the hot summer in southern California which is not blessed with raindrops enough to soften the ground one iota, and for some strange reason, digging the first one seemed to make such a very great impression on those of experience that very few victims ever dug a second one. Thank God that I never ever had to participate in that terrible punishment.

In the wartime army, it needs to be said at this point that enlisted men are not privy to top echelon planning, nor may they at liberty to even ask. But for some strange reason, soon came the day we were called to "fall out" at which time we were told that we were going to be moved to another location. I had a gut feeling that something was brewing because things had been too darned quiet around Topside for too long. So now it was happening, and, of course, no mention of where the location was to be; another "secret" bit of information.

So we all readied our respective items of interest and were escorted down to the railroad siding there on the main base. "Topside", as the staging area was called, soon became only a memory.........good for some and bad for others.

The long troupe train was loaded with our things: trucks and mobile guns to the front of the string of flat cars, and other stuff in boxcars aft, followed by troupe train "Pullman" cars fully equipped with stacked army cots (three high). Again all windows were blackened and we were told to leave everything we had seen behind and to keep our mouths closed and speak to no one about anything military, "...for the walls have ears."

The engineer sounded the steam whistle and we began our journey through the night to places unknown. This time we passed through no major towns that would provide a clue as; to our location. But the next day as we steamed along, I did recognize where we were because I had visited friends in that area during a couple of my leave weekends away from the base. We were headed north through the San Joaquin valley. Occasionally the train would stop for a while for some reason, and the guys would hand letters which they had written to folks back home to by bystanders to mail for them.

The area near Bend, Oregon proved to be our destination, at least by train. We stopped on a logging railroad spur deep into the piney woods where we spent a few days off-loading our equipment onto the ground. On to the north! By truck convoy.

Fort Lewis, Washington was a beautiful army base, but guess what! It didn't appear to be our future home! We drove right on through to another "staging" area. Right out into the woods! It did nothing but rain right straight down. It did. Day after day it rained. **AND** it was so foggy one could hardly see the ground they happened to be standing on. But neither fog or snow or rain nor hot sun seemed to interfere with the United States Army! "...onward Christian Soldiers..."

The Command had organized everyone into two "armies": the "red" army and the "blue" army. I think we wound up being in the blue army. Any way they held a mock invasion and had things appearing very real: Airplanes, helicopters Guns firing blanks, infantrymen, and the like. WE LOST. The Red army left for port of embarkation supposedly destined (according to gossip) for the Pacific Theater of operations. We were sent back to Camp Irwin (now Ft. Irwin) to do our basic training all over again, we were told. Actually, we wound up at Muroc Field (Edwards AFB) to stand guard over the flight testing of the prototype B-32 and the B-29 bombers.

It was a beautiful morning there in the Mojave Desert on that Saturday, and since it wasn't a workday, I figured I would go take a leisurely shower and do my laundry at the same time. That had proven to be a very efficient and easy to do one's laundry and many guys made use of their shower in that way. Having finished that part of my latrine chore, I proceeded to shave and return to the 8-man tent (typical for those of us who were considered temporary residents of a permanent military base. As I was about to wash my razor and put it away, I glanced into the mirror in front of me above the sink, and guess who I spotted right beside me...a buddy who had shipped out overseas just a few weeks prior. Yeah! One of the guys of the red army who had gone on that ship overseas.

Well I was totally shocked! Here was a guy who was supposed to be somewhere in the pacific fighting on an island or something. "Eddie" (not his real name) "...Where in the heck did you come from? I thought you..." "Yeah, Easley, we did! We shipped out on one of those "Victory ships". But when we got a couple of days out from Bremerton, a Jap sub torpedoed us and the ship went down. Lot of guys got into lifeboats and made it OK, but most went down with the ship. So we were picked up, and here I am. I'm waiting to be reassigned."

"Oh, my gosh! Well I sure am glad you made it, but them other guys...? Sure is sad, and to think about their folks at home."

I never saw him again, but he's still in my prayers.

This, as far as I know never appeared in any newspaper nor on any radio newscast. There were numerous other catastrophic incidents which never were made public. So neither shall I discuss them here.

Round number two: My second trip to the hospital; same hospital, same procedures, different doctors, different scenario. However, the procedures and outcomes were similar and the side effects are the same. The only thing, this time after three months, I was given a medical honorable discharge from the army and sent home.

The hard part was that I had made a few civilian friends who had come to visit me, and it was hard for me to say my goodbyes to them all. But I did plan to get on that greyhound bus and head out with my two barracks bags bulging with all my earthly possessions.

CHAPTER 16
* * *
CIVILIAN-LIFE ANEW

Since the war was still in progress, things on the outside were different. Actually, I didn't really know what the differences were. All I really knew were those things I had been told in letters from home and by those friends who I had made locally. But here I was at the bus station with all my things and not a soul in sight that I knew, and it was 200 miles to the nearest town where friends lived. So I pulled out my wallet and invested eleven of my precious few dollars in a ticket to Earlimart, California. I didn't return to Albuquerque because I needed to save all my money possible because it was that I had no job to go to and I had no prospects of one any time soon. So that's why I decided to go to the friend's town. Well not exactly the real reason. Actually, Erma's folks had moved to Earlimart and had gone to work on a farm there. So there's where I headed.

Of course, they were all happy to see me, especially in civilian clothes! I, too, was equally happy; to see them.

As the following week passed I had managed to speak to the publisher of the Delano newspaper who, upon hearing of my recent discharge from the army, offered to run an editorial telling of my situation and that I was planning to open a radio repair shop in the local Delano Hardware store. Needless to say any more. People responded in large numbers and I had more work than I could handle and soon found myself three months behind. All were happy, though, since no other radio repair shop was nearby, and new radios were nonexistent because the war situation resulted in no new cars, new radios, new anything for the general public. So we fixed up the old ones and were more than happy to do so and help win the war.

Erma and I soon became accustomed to being together again and rented a small but nice single bedroom house in Delano and I settled into my new job. The Thomson Music Company who owned and operated a chain of juke boxes and slot machines there locally paid me a visit one day at my shop and offered me a business proposition. Of course, I was a bit naive, but not completely stupid. I knew right away he was trying to get rid of his potential competition since he had a shop but no radio repairmen. So he made me an offer to take me into his shop as his radio repairman and also wanted me to take on the job of keeping his juke boxes going. After due consideration I did accept his offer because he promised to send me to school in Los Angeles to the Wurlitzer Company to bone up on that type of work. I would never afford to do something like that on my own with my meager income. It worked out very well, and things started looking very good for Erma and me.

Soon we were blessed with a son in January of 1945: James Forrest Easley. But as more time passed I resigned there and accepted a job with CBS at the Voice of America Radio station as a security guard. This offered me the opportunity to work among the fifteen radio engineers there and learn more about electrical engineering. This was good because at my salary, I would never be able to attend university to learn that profession.

In the few months to come, the war ended and the security guard job was done away with and I had to accept the janitorial job at the Radio station which was available. But in a few months that job ended too and I did whatever I could find to do.

So Ed and I bought a hay baler from a friend and contracted to bale alfalfa hay for several farmers which totaled about 700 acres every month. We operated that business for a year or so and made quite a nice nest egg to return to Albuquerque and start life anew. That's when I made a decision to change careers completely. I went to the Veterans Administration people and was tested to determine my aptitude capabilities. It turned out I was a natural, they said, for watchmaking, electrical engineering, or cabinetmaking. WOW! Cabinetmaking!

I hadn't even thought about that before, but that really rang a bell and I signed up for a cabinetmaker's apprenticeship under the master cabinetmaker, Joe Gibbons. Joe interviewed me and I began training in his shop in January, 1947, graduating in 1951 as a journeyman cabinetmaker.

However, just prior to my graduation from this apprenticeship, we were blesses again. A beautiful daughter which I helped deliver upon her entry into this life: Margaret Carol Easley. (As it happened, we were turned away at the St.. Joseph Catholic hospital there in Albuquerque because it was that I didn't have the fifty dollars up front they required to be admitted; I only had forty five dollars to my name. So we returned home after I had called our doctor to update him on the situation. He agreed to meet us at our home for the delivery, which was near at hand. Well, as it turned out, the baby arrived before the doctor, so I proceeded with the delivery. The doctor arrived just in time for the baby's first bath and the cutting of the cord.)

Then, within a year or so, Erma decided she would spread her wings and begin seeing another man, an Air Force sergeant. This, sad to say, led to her going away with him and leaving me with the kids while I was on work assignment in Santa Fe for the cabinet shop. A neighbor called me at my work place and informed me of the situation and that she was baby-sitting the kids. So I returned home and retrieved the kids and made arrangements to care for them. Things were under control and I was informed that Erma was pregnant from her new-found lover and had sued for divorce. But I had to go on with my life and raise the kids the best I could. So I had a talk with Ed and they agreed to help me care for them while I worked, for which I was extremely grateful.

I continued working in that capacity at the cabinet shop until I contracted meningitis in spring of 1951 and was reduced to being a total vegetable for a long while. It took several years and the love of my mother and my brother, Don, to help me through it.

But another tragedy equally as heartbreaking stuck its ugly head up which changed both my life and the lives of both of my two children. At first I was confined to an isolation hospital room at the Veterans Administration Hospital there in Albuquerque which totally prevented me from even seeing or talking to the children. Necessarily I was forced to leave them with their grandparents, Ed and his wife, by mutual agreement, until I would recover enough that I could return home and have the kids with me. However, while I was lying there in my isolation-room hospital bed and confined in the hospital, Ed and his wife decided to take both the kids and move to California to be near their two other daughters, without even a word to me to say they were doing this. Many weeks later I had recovered to the point that I was released and did in fact return home to recuperate. But it was after my return home that I learned where Ed had gone with my two kids. Since I was not a fellow with the fortune a lawyer would require to sue him for kidnaping, I had no choice but to shed my millions of tears and to live alone.

Forrest and His Two Oldest Children: James (Jim)
Forrest and Margaret Carol Easley (1952).

Don was told of all this and offered to have me move to Boulder, Colorado into his home until I was well enough to be on my own again. I did! I accepted his offer since I figured that I had no choice in the matter. They were very gracious and loving and accepted me into their home at no cost to me and I did quite well even though I missed my children terribly. As the months rolled by and grew into about two years I had recovered sufficiently for Don to find a helper type job for me in the Westinghouse appliance store in Boulder, Colorado. Don was a very successful and quite talented watchmaker there on Pearl Street and had established himself quite well both business wise and socially and had many good friends. So I was included into their social lives as well. This was something that had never happened to me; being included into the social circle of another family, especially my own relatives. But here I was being included in most everything they did socially and as a result I was introduced to many people and, therefore, made many good friends, some of which became special.

Also the Rook family, owners and managers of the Westinghouse dealership where I was working included me into their social circles. As a result, my self-esteem and outlook on the future was improving.

It was a blessing from Heaven that Don welcomed me into his home with his wife, Dorothy, and young 4-year-old son with no strings attached to allow me to have ample time to heal and have family around me so I would not be all alone in Albuquerque. Well to tell the truth, I really didn't any longer have my home there on south second because it was that I had lost my job due to my prolonged illness and the bank had foreclosed and was taking my home away. So I tried to salvage what equity I had in it somehow. Interestingly, I was told one day at the local country store that the store owner's sister was getting married and would be looking for a place to live. Her husband was in the Air Force and stationed there at Kirtland AF base. So, as if out of the blue, the thought occurred to me to let that couple have my house and let them keep up my mortgage payments until it was paid for. It would become theirs. I had the loan paid down to $4700, so that's all they would need to pay off. So they agreed and paid me $30 per month for my equity until their payments were finished, at which time it became their house. We agreed and did just that. It went well and all concerned were happy.

I worked as I felt like it at the appliance store and gradually improved and eventually began working a full 40-hour week. I made new friends and life seemed to get a bit better for me, even though my two children had been hauled off to California by their grandparents during my infirmity. Never again was I able to have them with me since they being out of state prevented me from having anyway to get them back. I was not a rich person and lawyers come high. So all those things just added to my life's sad experiences: Wife running off with an air force man; my two kids stolen from me.

Time passed. I slowly healed. I had learned to talk again somewhat and my memory had started to be retrained a bit. This is when another friend took charge and convinced me to attempt entering college and use it as therapy to retrain my brain because a good portion of it had been damaged to the point of almost no memory at all and very little speech capability. He suggested I enroll at Colorado State University which was only seventy miles away, and commit to a forestry major at once. This is a very technical major which requires an extreme amount of anatomical memorization of all the trees and their dendrology, and plants and insects as well as all their diseases. Then there were mathematics and physics and a host of other subjects such as silviculture, statistical analysis, seeding and planting, logging and milling, soils, chemistry, geology, law, civil engineering, technical writing, and many more for a total of 74 subjects to be learned. It scared me half to death to even think of taking on such a task, especially in my condition. But he told me it would retrain my brain totally. He was a forester himself and a graduate of both Princeton University and the University of Michigan. He also held a master's degree in forestry and had forty seven years of work experience with the Department of Agriculture dating back to Theodore Roosevelt for whom he worked in the beginning.

But I needed some time to think this over. He was suggesting something that seemed insurmountable to me, a simple country person who always had dreamed of such a future, but never had the opportunity or courage or money to pursue it. Also, I was a very timid person from the very beginning; how could I jump into such a complicated situation as this. So I chose to wait a while and mull it over.

One day at the store, Mrs. Rook took a phone message which she passed immediately on to me since I happened to be standing nearby. It seemed this customer of theirs needed to buy a television set and have it installed complete with an antenna. She thought I needed to handle this sale for the experience and to meet that family. So, being the obedient soul that I was, I loaded the necessary things into the company truck and drove out to their country residence. I must say I was very pleasantly pleased with the folks and their hospitality. Such a nice visit. The folks were quite elderly and the lady was mostly blind but ever so sweet----the husband no less cordial and nice. After finishing the installation, they would have it no other way except that I come to dinner the next evening after work. I accepted. That is when my life took another big turn----- for the better.

When I arrived, guess what? YEP! You are ahead of me aren't you? Their granddaughter, Joan, was there and was introduced to me and was seated next to me at the dinner table. (I later learned that this was a "set up" by the grandparents to have their granddaughter meet some nice man, since she was twenty four and single.) The meal was perfect. It was of a professional chef, although Mr. Hoar had prepared it himself, but I found that Joan was even more special than the meal. Such a nice person, and so pretty. She was a few years younger than I, and very nicely groomed and had class most girls don't possess. Needless to say we "clicked" and were soon dating.

Months went by and we decided we needed to be together as a couple so we became engaged and were married the following June. But the question still remained about me entering college. Joan and I discussed it very thoroughly. She agreed that I should do this and that she would be at my side all the way and help me through the rough spots.

So I did! I took Sam up on it, and did just that! But I must say It turned out fine, but in the beginning I found it the most difficult thing I had ever tangled with. But with his and Joan's constant support and kindness, I stuck it out and did graduate and did receive my Bachelor of Science Degree in June, 1958. But above all, I am so grateful that God had blessed me with His Grace and has led me all the way to a good life despite many obstacles which have fallen across my path. Along the way, however, Joan and I were blessed with two sweet children, Victoria Joan and David Michael.

CHAPTER 17

*   *   *

AT LAST!

June 8, 1958

The day arrived! It was graduation day and Joan and Mom were at my side. But one must know that all was no bed of roses getting there, but many, many wonderful experiences are remembered as well. The first day as a freshman has to be mentioned since it described my entire life up to that point as a shy, and very timid person. I suppose one can accurately say that these characteristics are what kept me from reaching some sort of successes along the way in life up that point. Here's what happened on that memorable (to me) day, my first day in college.

Actually, I cannot say it was the first day *in* college because it was that I didn't show up on campus that day. When I got up that morning, I was extremely nervous about starting school at age 30 among all those "high school" graduates: those 19-year-olds. I had no idea what lay in store for me that day. I figured it would be a day of complete strangers who I had no clue as to who they were and did not want them staring at ME the "old man." So I went for a walk instead of driving that 70 miles to my first class. I walked up into the hills west of Boulder and sat on a huge flat rock. I sat there trying to figure how to explain my feelings and actions to those back at the house. But after a couple of hours, I had a good excuse to not go to school that day; I would be very late because it was a 70-mile drive. Fine!

Next morning I got ready and made the trip to Ft. Collins to the

campus of Colorado State University, reported in, and, "OH, no....
Guess what!" I mumbled to myself. Yep! You guessed it! I had it figured
all wrong! **This** was the first day! Sure was!

I was put into the group of new freshmen to be given the tour of the
campus and to gather in a large room and proceed to introduce ourselves
to each other. This is exactly the reason I had stayed in Boulder the
day before: so I would miss having to do this thing. Boy! Now I really
did get nervous. We had to line up alphabetically and, since my last
name started with an "E", I was placed quite a ways down the line of
the "circle". The first freshman student gave their name and where they
were from and their major. As progression was made, the next person
had to repeat the information from the first person and add their own,
and so on. I was probably the 20th person down the line and I could
see right away . . . .

By the time it came my turn, there had been so much to remember,
and I had this memory problem anyway . . . .

So I just decided to fess up and tell them this was an impossible thing
for me, that I would just tell them that information that pertained only
for myself. That is what I did. I felt ever so much better when the next
person followed MY lead and did the same thing. I left there figuring
the whole idea was a psychological gimmick conjured up by that female
guide, a junior, I think.

Well, so much for that morning!

We had been given handouts which included a map of the campus
with a number-coded identification listing thereon of the most
important buildings we would need to memorize in due time. At the
moment, however, I was interested only in a place to grab a sandwich
and something to wash it down with. I scanned the map briefly and
low and behold I spotted the "student Union building" listed, and I
set out to physically locate it on the ground and to satisfy my hunger
pangs. It turned out that every other student on that very busy campus
had the same idea as I, which resulted in a major pedestrian traffic jam
to say the least.

This was followed by a scheduled all hands assembly for the incoming
freshmen class in the gymnasium for a welcoming address by the college
president. Now this was IT! I was already getting in the swing of it all

and started to "feel" like a college student, at least I thought I did. But since the next few days and weeks added a bit more doubt, I decided to just tough it out and try to survive. It was going to be a real bear to accomplish those things I needed to accomplish in order to become "one of them." However, though, when classes actually started and I began to familiarize myself with the building locations and the short "ten minutes" between classes and how to take proper notes, It all made a little more sense. Then came the "tests." I think the taking of those tests and seeing for myself that I l did as well or better than the incoming freshmen "kids" (remember I was 30 years old compared to their 18- and 19-year ages). I began taking stock of my life and put into perspective all my life's experiences and training and learning during those fourteen years since high school. I soon realized I had a bit of an edge on the younger folks. So my self-esteem began improving and I found myself doing very well indeed in my studies.

My memory began returning. In fact I found that much of what I had learned in earlier life was now beginning to return and was becoming a base for my new learning experiences. For example, one of my required classes in the forestry major was mechanical and architectural drafting. In retrospect, during my cabinetmaker apprenticeship there in Albuquerque under Joe Gibbons, I was required to master those same drafting abilities. So at the outset of the drafting class there at the College of Forestry at CSU, Dr. Carl Newport (happened he was my same age) noticed right away my talents and asked me to assist him in teaching the Lab session of his drafting classes which were to be taught on Tuesdays and Thursdays. Of course, I was delighted and quite pleased with myself in that I had recovered enough to actually do this thing. (As a matter of fact, that was the only A+ grade I ever made in college.) It also was very beneficial in curing my shyness and changing my bashful personality. And so it went. I actually was asked later on during my sophomore year to assist in teaching Forest Dendrology and during my junior year to assist in teaching Advanced Forest Economics. Those experiences really gave me the confidence that I had never had earlier in life. I think these experiences were key in turning my life around from a person being satisfied with being a "regular" laboring type person to a Professional person and a leader anxious to learn and learn and learn.

I still possess those qualities and to the day of this writing continue to learn: The more difficult, the more I dig into it!

College went actually better than I had figured it would. I learned much and made so many friends. This fact alone was a blessing because since I had been stricken with meningitis I had made no new friends to speak of. In fact most of the old friends from the years past had either moved on or passed away and left me sort of in a start-over mode. Making new friends was a very precious accomplishment, especially at this point in my life.

It seems that these four years spent in "curing myself" from my brain damage and re-learning most everything had done even more than serve as therapy for my loss of memory. It seemed to me that it had provided me with a 4-year "rest" from the real world and gave me a brand new way of life: A *new* Forrest Easley! I was a different person. It is true that in the days of the past, my brain processes were of "lightning speed" so to speak, and I had a near photographic memory to boot. But as a result of the brain damage, resulting from the illness, and even after this four-year period and the retraining of my old brain and the new areas of my brain, my thought processes are probably normal but quite a bit slower, however, retention is permanent. Once learned, a thing is forever engraved upon my brain. But, I find it much more difficult to learn a new thing. I do have to explain to whomever is interested that majoring in this extremely difficult major of forestry does require an extreme amount of memorization and logic training. I spent many years since graduation in professional research investigation and medical studies as well as military weapons research and design, and found the memorization required in forestry much more demanding than any of those. My mentor, Sam Detweiler, who guided me through all this, truly knew what he was talking about and had guided me exactly in the proper direction. My true appreciation will always be of him. Thank you, Sam! (Sam passed from this life just prior to my graduation.)

Graduation day saw me as one very tired and worn-out human being, I dare say. I, toward the end of my senior year, had thoughts of continuing on to work on a Master's Degree. However, I just didn't have enough energy left to accomplish that large task, so I put that idea on hold for the moment. Graduation day (June 8, 1958) was a very great day for me. I had managed to accomplish what seemed many times along the way to be an impossible thing for me to complete. Additionally, I had, over that four-year stint at the university, proven to myself that I could do the impossible. I had stuck it out and worked at four part time jobs to pay the bills and tuition and books and so on, not to mention to actually earn a very difficult college degree in spite of my handicap. I was and am very proud of myself in that respect. As a result, life has been so much better and my professional job successes immediately improved unbelievably.

During my junior and senior years, various corporations and the Department of Agriculture sent many recruiters to the universities of interest to interview those prospective graduates for employment by their particular organization. I, thereby, had opportunities to sit face to face and ask questions that had needed answers. Also, I was asked many questions by the recruiters which turned out to be a very important part of my training and, personally, a great part of my own life experience. Never before had I had such a wonderful and important opportunity to actually sit one-on-one with a real corporate representative to discuss my professional future. This was no doubt one of the best things that ever happened during my education and to my recovery from my handicap. I actually accepted this experience as a real part of my professional education and seriously treasure it to this day.

I was hired by my first interviewer and was sent an official letter of acceptance together with instructions pertaining to how to properly proceed preparing the remaining personnel paperwork, job location, and physical examination procedure. The new professional position, the first of my life, was to be in the city of Flagstaff, Arizona. I would be assigned to the Flagstaff District of the Coconino National Forest as the Timber Management and Reforestation Specialist. My first project was the reforestation of a large burned-over area west of Flagstaff that had been denuded of the Ponderosa Pine timber as a result of a hot box on a freight car axle. The freight car had been pulled over and dropped off on a siding with the cotton wadding on that axle on fire. The train crew had removed the burning wadding from the axle bearing and left it on the gravel near the tracks before continuing on with the train. It is surmised the wind blew the burning cotton waste onto nearby grass and fire spread, as a result, into the timber. Of course the railroad company paid for the damage. I hired a crew and hand planted many thousands of seedlings to replace the timber stand which had burned.

This was a very successful project. Today, I'm pleased to report this area displays a beautiful scientifically planted and spaced and managed Ponderosa Pine forest along Interstate 40.

CHAPTER 18

* * *

NEW CHALLENGES----- NEW HEART BREAKS

A few months passed and my new duties were quickly learned, and I began to feel a part of the U.S. Forest Service. Yes! I am now a real college graduate, a thing I never in my life before had even considered a remote possibility. Not only that, but here I was actually working in a real professional position as an actual professional forester. WOW! It struck me that, "Here I am. I am the first member of the Easley clan since the19th century to attend college and actually earn a real degree," I thought to myself. I just couldn't believe it at first. But as time passed and I continued to work among the other professionals, I began to feel as I was actually a part of that very well respected and responsible world of real scientists. This I found truly really humbling and it gave me that new feeling of "just beginning". I remember one of my professors at the university said to us one day just prior to graduating, "Some of you might leave here and think you know everything there is to know, but just remember that you have just begun to learn the basics. You are to leave here as a beginner with an open mind and heart to learning how the real world functions and prosper from its teachings and experiences, and appreciate the enormity of the things that lie ahead."

Things began to get very realistic very quickly. For example, one of the first things to bring me to reality was the telephone call I received one evening after dinner. It was the fire dispatcher with a message for me telling me that I was needed in California with my fire crew of twenty five Hopi Indians to join hundreds of others to help fight a large project fire at Nuhall just north of Los Angeles. This was a mandatory thing. So I met him at the Knob Hill USFS (U.S. Forest Service) dispatcher's office and was transported immediately to Holbrook, AZ to meet the TWA Constellation Passenger plane which we turned around at Albuquerque to fly back to Holbrook to pick us up and take us to the Glendale airport to connect with further transport to the fire line.

While we were waiting for the plane to return from Albuquerque, We signed up the twenty five Hopi firefighters and had them ready to board the plane. There were four of us liaison officers each in charge of twenty five firefighters who boarded that plane.

This was my first official fire-fighting assignment, but in reality it turned out to be much more. We were led to the fire line on foot by the Assistant District Ranger at approximately midnight local time. It was extremely dark except for the light from the huge flames from the burning scrub oak brush. We were issued hard-hat electric headlamps, but there weren't enough to go around. Some of us had to work without one. As the person in charge of my crew, I was responsible for their safety plus everything else pertaining to them. Then a terrible thing occurred: As the men were extremely involved in knocking down those flames, a sudden gust of wind brought the fire so quickly up the small ravine that it engulfed two of the Hopi men. One jumped to safety, but the other tripped and fell into the fire and was cremated . . . . right in front of me. I ran forward to rescue him, but the flames surrounded me as well and I could not reach the poor man. There was nothing to do but to retreat, sadly. In doing so I ran into a barbed wire fence in the darkness and darn near fell into the fire myself. I realized that the fire had to be knocked down as soon as possible, so I continued with the men to knock the flames down to prevent them from reaching the gasoline refinery a few hundred yards away. This was a very tough decision to make, but make it I did. The man was already dead and there remained nothing to do to save him. He was already gone and burned. In California, at that time, it was a legal requirement that the dead person had to remain in place and not be touched by anyone until the coroner arrived. This took a good four hours for him to travel from downtown Los Angeles. So I had to meet with the Indians' tribal leader and arrange the procedure for transport of the remains according to Hopi customs, as well as continue knocking down that very hot fire. This was a very touchy subject with them because the Hopis would have nothing to do with a corpse. But, eventually, we agreed on an acceptable way to send him home to his family at Second Mesa, AZ where they lived. I also had to complete the insurance paperwork and all other things including his pay.

This is only one example of the many experiences a Forester must endure since he is the person who is the official federal administrator of the National Forest and all that goes on there.

Time went by. More was accomplished. Timber sales were planned, standing timber inventories were measured and recorded, and timber management plans were written. Also grazing management plans were written for those ranchers who were permitted to graze their cattle and sheep on the Coconino National Forest. Mining permits were issued and surveys made. Freeway construction permit applications were reviewed and negotiated, and rights of ways were regularly inspected for conformity with federal law and related civil engineering and survey data. Also, watershed management and permits with the city of Flagstaff were kept up to date together with the ski lift folks and their permits to operate on the slopes of the San Francisco Peaks north of town. It was a busy job and I loved it. As I iterated earlier, a forester is a well-educated person and must have quite a broad background in all the earth sciences, not to mention he must love mother nature and truly enjoy being out of doors.

But, per normal procedure, one gets transferred from one location to another to broaden one's experience base. So I was notified that my turn had arrived and that I was to be immediately transferred to the Beaver Creek District some sixty miles away as the new Assistant District Ranger. This, of course meant that I was being promoted and would be working on a District which comprised both timber land and desert land plus grazing lands. Also, I would function as the administrator of fifteen weather stations on the district and report the recorded data to the U.S. Weather service in Phoenix once a week on Monday. All this is not to mention that I was also the Fire Protection

Officer for the district. As such, it was part of my job to train and oversee our fire crews and teach fire-fighting techniques to the crews along with functioning as the District Safety Officer and held safety training class every Monday morning. All this was very interesting and quite a challenge. Also, as a side note, during the winter months most travel up in the high country of the timbered areas, a snow cat with tracks had to be used in to traverse the logging roads for access to the weather station sites and to carry out most other duties of my job. But I was very much at home in this element because I was brought up in the high snow country of New Mexico and had spent many happy hours in the wild mountainous country and the prairie lands during all types of weather and storms.

To digress back a bit to when I was assigned at working at Knob Hill, I had occasioned to work in conjunction with the fire dispatcher there and his secretary, Miss Vasquez, so now being at Beaver Creek, I still utilized them daily by radio as part of my routine work duties. It was like a family that all worked as a unit and occasionally had administrative banquets. So we all knew each other very well. But it seems that for some crazy reason, that old man "trouble" was about to raise his head again.

I give you three guesses what happened. YEP! Old trouble rolled its ugly eyes at me again. Wouldn't you know, just as my world was getting to be a wonderful experience, and my day had been a very fruitful and happy one, I went home after work all set to tell Joan of my great day, but ALAS! NO WIFE!! NO KIDS!! All I found was a note. It read: "Daddy came and got us and took us back to Boulder with him because Mother asked him to do it because she couldn't stand having her daughter so far away from her." Needless to say I was in total shock and couldn't believe what I was reading. I read the note again, and again.

Well this would require a very long story to explain, so I will just say that the extreme and great influence "Mother" possessed and exerted resulted in divorce and me remaining on the job at Beaver Creek. What next?? Why Me?? Wasn't I ever going to be permitted a happy life as are other men?

Forrest's Son, David Michael and Daughter, Victoria Joan, 1959

Needless to say, after all this my desire to work at the job was almost zero. All I wanted was to run get my family. I tried, but when I arrived, my car door was held shut when I arrived and I was asked to leave or else. So, knowing the details of just what "Mother" had done, I left.

Life was lonely. Work was difficult, but I realized I had to go on. I did. But my "work family" stood by me and included me in their off-work activities, so as time passed things grew a bit more bearable and my friends grew closer. As the months passed I realized my family had been transformed to just a lot of memories.

Work became more pleasant, actually enjoyable again, I began to live again and go places in off time and to visit my friends. I especially enjoyed being invited for "dinner", because that meant I didn't have to eat a TV dinner that night. I even dated a time or two. l guess one could call it dating when I asked a female friend at work whether she would mind driving to Phoenix with me to shop. Anyway, it amounted to a very nice day and other nice pleasantries such as great conversations and a movie or two.

CHAPTER 19
* * *
RELOCATING TO CALIFORNIA

Again, my unexplained forces were trying their best to change my destiny. It was a bit beyond me to put it all together in my mind. There was something surreal about it all, something like what one would dream in a weird dream. I gave this much serious thought from many viewpoints and concluded very little in the way of an answer. But life went on and work went on.

One evening after work, I was sitting in a Flagstaff café enjoying a soft drink when I was joined by the fire dispatcher's secretary, Miss Vasquez, Theresa, but we informally called her by her nickname, Terri. I invited her to sit down with me and visit. During our informal friendly chat, the thought occurred to me to share my thoughts with her about these changes that were happening in my life. Of course, she knew Joan and had heard of her leaving me to return to her mother in Boulder, taking the kids with her. That seemed to bother her more than anything else we were discussing. Right away she saw my pain of losing my family and offered her sympathy and empathy for which I thanked her and told her of my appreciation of her feelings.

As time passed, we talked again several times and she invited me to her parents' home for meals. They were from Mexico and, I must say, prepared excellent Mexican meals. Since I was raised in New Mexico, I have always been a person who loves Mexican food of all kinds. And once they learned of this, I was invited often and became a constant guest for dinner. Well, also, I came to know all of the living members of Terri's family, all thirteen of them, and soon became a guest at all their homes. I was accepted as one of them, and the fact that I did speak limited Spanish helped cement the bonds with them all. Naturally, Terri and I became much closer since we kind of worked together anyway, and soon started doing things together in our off times.

Then another interesting thing happened. I was visited at the office by one of my classmates who had accepted a position with the North Dakota Forest Service in Bottineau, North Dakota. His official business in Flagstaff was to obtain samples of live Limber Pine for use as specimens at the College of Forestry there in Bottineau. NOTE: The only two places that species of pine occurs is at the very top rim of the San Francisco Peaks at about 13,000 feet elevation, and at the top of the White Mountains near Mono Lake in eastern California. I drove up there in the Forest Service Jeep and obtained those specimens for him and packaged them with the federal plant-inspection certification indicated on the package.

The other thing he wanted was to recruit me as State Forester to be stationed there at the College of Forestry. My duties would be to teach forestry during the winter season and serve as State Forester as well. That sounded very fine to me, but only one hitch crossed my very active mind: The winters there are extremely cold. Normal temperature would be around minus 40 degrees F. However, I promised him I would give it great thought and would get back to him.

I discussed this situation with Terri to get her input, since we had become very close. Of course we both shared the same feeling about being separated like that. But we both agreed that I should not refuse that position as it might scar my future professional reputation. So I sent my acceptance on to Bottineau and made arrangements to move there ASAP. This placed Terri and me in a position of deciding what we were to do. So here, again, came this weird creature sticking its head up and trying to change my entire future. But we both knew the answer.

We drove to Las Vegas and were married and returned to Flagstaff to finish out her two weeks notification and mine too.

So we both submitted our resignations and prepared to make the big move even though it was December. We allowed an open-ended arrival time, and I must say it was a good thing we did, too! During our trip, we encountered major snow storms and road closures due to deep snow drifts and blizzards. We were snowed in at Cheyenne for a week and again at Custer for another two weeks. However we finally completed the trip with much trouble and icy road conditions the entire distance. At our arrival, it was minus 40 degrees F and we found it extremely difficult to locate an apartment and get unloaded into it.

We decided to check in at the office then spend the entire month ahead deciding whether this was for us. As it turned out, it wasn't the weather and cold temperature, that threatened, it was that we were not accepted because the "natives" there were of a very different ethnic background and were very *clickish* and would not let us "in," so to speak. I could see right away that should I ever be eligible for a promotion or a favor, that I would be ignored and passed over. So Terri and I packed up our belongings, and left notice of our decision to return to my position at Flagstaff. However, this was not to be. Upon arrival there, I found the position already filled. I had to find another source of income right away due to the great expense we had just had making that move. So we drove to Albuquerque and had a talk with Joe Gibbons at the cabinet shop. It just happened that he needed a temporary cabinet maker and put me to work right away. Terri also lucked out and found work at the Forest Service Regional office. This allowed time to look for permanent work somewhere.

After a bit of ad searching, I located a good position in San Carlos, California as a Technical Editor for the Lenkurt Electric Corporation, a subsidiary of General Telephone Corporation. I called, was interviewed, and hired with travel expenses paid. A week later, we were on the job on the new job and things looked very wonderful. It was just at Thanksgiving time, too, and the company passed out turkeys to all employees. That was a real treat for us since we were new arrivals and had nothing else established yet for celebrating the holiday.

Time passed again, but this time, we learned that Terri was expecting. So the following June, we were blessed with a beautiful daughter, Pamela Catherine. From the very beginning, she was Daddy's girl! This lasted until she celebrated her sixteenth birthday. Becoming "independent" certainly spoils and severs so many relationships. More on that sad subject later.

My job went well and I enjoyed many promotions and became

one of the company's liaison representatives with the Strategic Air Command during the building and outfitting the Atlas Missile silos. We manufactured and were the overseers of the installation of multiplexing telephone equipment into the silos and into certain B-52 aircraft for SAC. Not to belabor this point, but within about six years the company changed its retirement policies and began laying off professional people just prior to retirement time. This worried me no end. Of course, this was my plan: to retire and have an dependable income for life. So, again, I had to think of another change.

I, then, contacted the Federal Civil Service folks and obtained a listing of available Technical Editor Positions in the government. I applied and got onto the federal register, because it was that they chose their people from the register, giving veterans a five or ten point preference, depending upon whether they were disabled or not. A few months later, I was called into my supervisor's office to be told that I had an incoming phone call from the "government." Right there in his office I took the call and listened to what was told to me.

"Mr. Easley, this is the Personnel Manager at China Lake Naval Weapons Center near Ridgecrest, California. I am calling to advise you we have two Technical Editor openings which need filling very soon. Are you still available?"

"Yes sir!" I said. "Tell me more about them." He continued, "Well, one is on the staff of the Fleet Engineering Department, and the other is on the staff of the Technical Information Department." I replied, "I would want to interview both departments as soon as possible." He replied, "I will set it up and get back to you very soon." My supervisor looked at me and said to me, "Sounds like you are going to be leaving us, Forrest." I told him, "Yes, but it's not without tears because you folks have been so great as friends and so good to work with. I will miss all of you."

He did make the arrangements and, as promised, called me, and followed up by official memo stating the dates and times of the office appointments. I traveled there, had my interviews, and had my choice of either position. I chose the Fleet Engineering Department and was hired. My job description set forth my duties as required to provide Technical Writing and Editing for the many, many fleet engineers of

ALL disciplines and physicists, mathematicians, Chemical Research Scientists, Metallurgy engineers and metallurgical X-Ray Researchers, Solid State Engineers and Physicists, Computer design Physicists, Optical and Laser Physicists, and Avionics and Medical Researchers. My duties also included the scientific writing and technical writing required by the bomb and missile fusing and explosive research, and cryogenic scientists. Testing plans and test reports were also included in my huge menu of duty assignments. Needless to say, again, that this all sort of frightened me because of its magnitude of disciplines. But I have always been one to learn new and difficult things, so I eagerly looked forward to this new challenge.

The Navy moved us right away and gave us housing on the Navy base. It was an easy decision, even though I had to take a two thousand dollar cut in annual pay. However, in a couple of years I was back to more than my civilian salary there at Lenkurt.

CHAPTER 20
* * *
RETURN TO THE MOJAVE DESERT

My memory immediately recalled these familiar surroundings as the long-ago forgotten world which I lived in during WW2 during my Army days. Yes many of my days were spent performing my Army duties in so many various places all over this immense and boundless desert called the great Mojave (pronounced Mo-hah-vee) Desert. But I had always liked the desert, not as a military training area, but as a playground and a great place to explore, and, also, the warm to hot weather conditions. Yes! I do love the desert. I especially enjoy very much traveling around the desert during the early spring and observing the millions of wild flowers. It seems that God has placed every species of blooming plant there and programmed them to live together in planned colonies of their own kind. Such beauty, and it, sadly, is unknown and un-observed by most.

My work at the Navy research laboratory there was mostly classified, but I will say that working with those 4,400 world class scientists was an incomparable experience second to none that one could possibly be a part of elsewhere. It was a totally different world, yet a world where everyone was a close friend with the next person, even though we were all separated assignment wise by "need to know" security classifications.

*Forrest Explains To the A-4 Fighter Pilot the New
Modifications Made To the Weapon-Release System*

However, a distinct thing existed with almost every one of us was
that we were all involved deeply and intimately with the design and
development and implementation of military weapons of war, and truly
realized that those weapons would sometime be used to affect peoples'
lives negatively. As a result, most everyone attended those many chapels
and churches of the area and tended to live above average Christian lives
with heart-felt sincerity. This alone made it well worth the opportunity
to be there and be a part of nice group of fellow workers . . . . .and
they were all professional, about three fourths with doctorates if I had
to guess.

Navy housing was provided because the base was situated deep
in the desert and away from city-type housing, therefore, we enjoyed
many benefits one couldn't have off-base. First, there was a commissary
(supermarket) and a gas station, both of which did not charge federal
tax which made prices much lower, and the Navy security police and
fire departments, which were very, very efficient and always on the job
so to speak. Also we had a Navy hospital on base, located just across the
street from our duplex. Also, I lived only about a quarter mile from my
office, which allowed me to walk to work each day and return home
for lunch as well. I readily became "spoiled" to these benefits and truly

enjoyed my time there which amounted to approximately fourteen and a half years.

Along the way, again, we were blessed with two sons, Stephen Forrest and Matthew Christopher about six years apart, Matthew being the youngest. So now we were parents with my new family of three children and things seemed to go very well. The kids grew and schooling kept advancing, ever so quickly, it seemed. They were getting older and activities seemed to consume their every spare moment. Pam with her violin and piano lessons and, later on, Junior United Nations activities; Stephen with his clarinet lessons and boy scouts, then ham radio lessons and licensing; Matthew with his piano and violin lessons and baseball. He was getting quite known for his first-baseman abilities and played most every game. Also, I almost forgot to mention that Terri was taking piano lessons as well.

Now, it must be mentioned at this point that these music lessons were not available on the Navy base nor in the local town of Ridgecrest, nor were they inexpensive. NO!

I had to drive them all to Hollywood every Saturday to the Sherman School of Music, then, later to other music schools as they advanced. Mmm huh. 160 miles each way . . . . every Saturday . . . for ten years! Yes! And I wore out three cars doing it, not to mention the dollars it cost for the gas, the meals while there, the *shopping* which just had to be done. Oh, yes, and old dad got to just sit and listen to them and then afterward go enjoy those great lunches at the fine cafeteria there on Colorado Boulevard. WOW! What a place to eat fine food! Good thing I had a good job, wasn't it?

Chapter 21

MEMORIES FROM NWC

nwc!! That's the abbreviation used by the U.S. Navy to describe the Navy base at China Lake, California. Actually, the real name of the facility was: Naval Weapons Center.

The almost-restored 1928 Buick opera coupe was readied and was more than ready to begin the 500-or-so-mile trip from our home in San Carlos to the naval base at China Lake to get settled in to begin my new position there in the Fleet Engineering Department as the Department Technical Editor. I was to drive the old Buick and take Pam with me. Terri would drive the '60 Valiant station wagon and let Stephen ride in back to play or sleep as he chose. The night passed quickly as we took the back roads in order to stay off the main freeway. We arrived at the main gate of the base just after sunup on June 6th, 1966.

I checked in with security and was directed to the housing office and our new residence. This was to be a totally new experience for the entire family, and especially for Terri since she had never experienced any type of military life at all. But the family became quickly adjusted and life anew began, new friends were made, and new activities were soon discovered, and all was well.

My work was extremely interesting and diverse. As mentioned, my duties were very complex and included partnering with all of the various scientific and technical disciplines involved with researching and developing the navy weapons and weapons systems and making them operational and the training of the personnel who use them. A "Rocket Scientist"? Most say that. However, also, the writing and preparation and publishing the technical manuals and scientific reports involved were a part of my responsibilities. It goes without saying that most of this work was classified; the exit-gate sign on the base said: "WHAT YOU SAW HERE STAYS HERE."

Forrest Readies a 1,000-Pound Snake eye Bomb For Tail Fin Flight Testing.

Our children continued their education at the Navy-owned schools there on base, for which I have nothing but praise for their system of education, the high degree of qualifications of the teachers, **high** the high level of knowledge imparted to the students. The graduates from those schools were very bright and it showed. After all, the population of the base were 4,400 of the world's most intelligent scientists and engineers who actually demanded outstanding schools. The wives were also highly educated some of which were scientists as well. So it stood to reason their children were equally well educated and trained in ways of that social and scientific level. In fact, I was quite fortunate that my own children could be included in those schools as well.

Then, again, as time passed certain things seemed to change. Terri was diagnosed with cancer of the womb. She, after a talk with her doctor, decided she wanted to have another child before she would have to have it removed. So we discussed it and decided in the affirmative. Matthew was born to us with no adverse problems on April 20, 1969. He had all ten fingers and ten toes so to speak, and Terri had her womb removed successfully. No more cancer, no radiation or chemo treatment. We decided that to remove the cancerous womb would remove the cancer. We were correct and was proven by her living another forty four cancer-free years. She passed away in 2011 from an overly-prescribed pain medication. But back to the story.

Time marched on! All of the family started music lessons at the Sherman School of Music in Hollywood. This meant we had to get up a bit early to arrive at the school for the scheduled classes at eight AM every Saturday. We did that. We did; a 160-mile drive each way. For ten years we did. But, as before in my life, old man trouble stuck up his head again. He did! First, Terri decided she wanted to not be married anymore to me. She had become a bit too close with her piano teacher in Los Angeles and filed for divorce and moved to Pasadena. A bit later Pam, who was attending Occidental College in Glendale, dropped her advanced violin lessons to switch to a law major where her new boyfriend was studying.

Pamella Easley and Her Stradivarious Violin.

This was, to say the least, was very heart-breaking to the rest of the family because after we had gone to a world of financial and family denial to give her those ever-so-important violin lessons and the violin. Also there was the huge accomplishment of becoming a concert violinist who had not only performed at Carnegie Hall, but had also been on a month-long concert tour of Europe with a symphony orchestra and choir by age sixteen. This, not to mention that I had already purchased for her a very expensive Stradivarius violin. We had a long and unhappy discussion on the subject which I found to be a waste of my breath. She went on to earn a PhD Degree in International Law and is currently quite successful to say the least.

So this left Matthew and myself alone since Stephen was talked into staying with his mother in Pasadena.

Forrest's Son, Stephen, at the Steinway Piano in Concert.

This, of course, turned out to be another heart breaker. Steve drifted into the "wrong" set of "friends" and got into drugs. You can guess the end of that story: Dropped out of college, ended up in prison for a 6-year stay. Of course this totally destroyed any opportunities for a successful future as a concert pianist for which he was well trained; as well as Pam was with her violin.

All this was a burdensome heart breaking stress for me and, together with all the pressures of my job, a serious heart attack befell me one evening after retiring to bed. This proved to be the end of my working career. I asked God many times, "Why ME, God, why ME?" Then one night as I slept I awoke and pondered that question. It came to me. "Why NOT me." That's how I leave it, why not me?

*Forrest's Son, Matthew Christopher Easley on His
Graduation Day rom Washburn University.*

After a short recuperation, during which time had used up all my
sick leave and funds, I had to move from the navy base housing. So
Matthew and I managed to repair my old '56 Ford truck and load what
was left of my things after the divorce, borrow money for the move
from Mom, and move to Missouri. This trip had to be done a bit at a
time as I was still very weak from my 'bout with the heart attack. But
after a month of short trips eastward on I-40, we finally arrived at out
40 acre jungle here in Ozark County.

This, again, was a completely new beginning. We had come to a
complete un-improved, un-cleared acreage of Ozark wilderness under
grown with brambles thorn trees and poison ivy poison oak, poison

sumac, and other things, not to mention copper heads, ticks, chiggers, and a host of other things we had never encountered in the past.

This began a totally new story in my life.

Forrest's Son David Michael All Grown Up s a Proffessional Classical Guitarist. At Age 39, He passed Away As a Result of Incorrect Back-Pain Prescription.

I Had a Dream

Forrest N. Easley — 1974

It was then, so long ago, a dream I had
Of Heaven, peace on earth, love, serinity; yes, and a wife.
A wife with which to share children that love, that grow;
That learn, that cry, that pamper, that give me life.
Yes, I had a dream, a beautiful dream I had.

I dreamed a dreamer's dream, I suppose.
A home, success, a farm, a whispering brook
Running through the backyard of my life.
Visions of silvery dew on the morning grass and the rose,
The rush of the wind; nature's own storybook.

But it isn't meant to be — the gifts from God,
The fruits of toil, of sweat, of tears, of love.
Why must life be so cruel, so selfish
As to ignore the some and put others above?
Why am I not as worthy or deserving as they?

It wasn't meant for good to come my way,
Especially after I gave, and gave, and gave, and prayed
That they might succeed. Even so, great ugliness seems to reign
Over all that's within me, and yet I continue to weigh
My chances — my realization of a dream delayed.

Why, as life's twilight nears, do all one's friends retreat
To collect within their own dreams; and I stand amid my shambles
And dare to contemplate my destiny and try to imagine whether
God, too, will not want it to be: my dream, a dreamers dream,
Then, the last true friend slowly withdraws to other friends meet?

And why does the child from me turn and not give love and life?
Why does it twist the tender heart from my very breast
And go its way so unconcerned and so brave?
Yes, Oh God! A beautiful dream so long ago I had
But now nothing's left for me — a lonely fool — but the grave.

EPILOGUE

This appended information is included as a part of this Autobiography because it is an important part of my life's experiences and should be shared with the reader. Also, it helps answer many of the long list of questions that have been asked pertaining to the "Miraculous" Staircase and just how it supports itself without a central support. I shall forever be grateful to the Loretto Catholic Sisters for asking me, a student of Forestry and Wood technology at Colorado State University, to do a study of the staircase.

This was done without fee or obligation of the sisters, but as a heartfelt gift to them.

Forrest N. Easley

A
STAIRWAY
FROM
HEAVEN
?

FORREST N. EASLEY

Forester/wood Technologist
Consulting Researcher

February 1997

A technical investigation of a wood specimen
from the famous Loretto Staircase
in the Chapel of Our Lady of Light, Santa Fe, New Mexico

PREFACE

First, let me say that I consider it a great privilege to be asked to do this study of the wood in this very special staircase. I have to say, also, that I, for many years, have stood in awe while viewing this most wonderful work of art and mechanics which required the very greatest skill a man could possibly attain with his hands and mind. Therefore, I have approached this study with a totally open mind, unbiased, and with the utmost honesty.

During my formal training as a scientist, it was impressed upon me very early that one absolutely *must* eliminate all personal feelings and bias from a study in order that it be truly a scientific study. So in that light, this work was carried out. The report itself is written in third person, as it should be. However, I chose to write this *preface* in first person thereby adding the warmth and personal mood so necessary here.

BACKGROUND. As a child, I grew up in New Mexico and came to be a part of the culture and people of the area. Religion was always a part of my background since my parents were both very good Christians and God was always present in our home. Our family always traveled together and made many trips to visit the old missions and towns around the state. Santa Fe was always the most fascinating and had the most, I thought, to draw me back; as a magnet draws a piece of iron unto itself.

During the very early fifties, I had the pleasure of being the guest of the Sisters of Loretto Academy and was told the entire story and history of the academy, the chapel and the "mysterious" staircase. I always found the story of "that little man" appearing to offer his efforts to provide the sisters with a long-needed staircase to the choir balcony very interesting and, in my case, entirely believable. You see, I have always believed in miracles, but usually examine the situation to determine just how the miracle was performed, or, if in fact, it is actually a miracle. However, it is not the purpose of this paper to determine whether or not the building of this staircase was a miracle, but to attempt to identify the wood used therein and to investigate the physics of the support mechanism. At a later date, a mathematical model and physical model shall be constructed and this report will be amended to include the findings thereof.

I shall not endeavor to repeat the story here, but I advise the reader to refer to the publication *The Inexplicable Stairs* written by Sister M. Florian, O.S.F.

I had the privilege of having a personal tour, one-on-one, of the premises and especially of the chapel and staircase. We spent most of an afternoon, the Mother Superior and I, in the chapel and *on* the staircase and in the choir loft. I got an excellent opportunity to experience firsthand the reverence of that most *holy* place. The entire chapel definitely manifests peace, and holiness, and the very presence of God is truly felt—even to this day! My most favorite spot in the chapel is in the pew just under Jesus' statue where He looks directly into my eyes with such love as I sit and look at Him. One can feel His *love* penetrating to the very center of one's being.

TECHNICAL. As to structure of the staircase, it comprises two complete revolutions (720 degrees) in its entire height which sits on a reinforced floor and is attached at the top to the choir-balcony joist with wooden pegs. The design of the staircase is that of a **double spiral** connected with steps. The "double spiral" comprises two wood stringers each constructed in a spiral form, however, the inner stringer (spiral) is almost two and a half feet smaller than the outer stringer (spiral). In this type of design, the inner stringer which spirals on approximately a one-foot radius, is of such small radius that the stringer acts as a very stiff spiral (or spring, if you will). (Note: The measurements I state here are only approximate and are not to be taken as accurate, but are used only for explanation of a structural principal.) In other words, it functions in a structural situation as as *almost solid* cylinder of wood (as would a wooden "pole").

However, the outer stringer (spiral) is of much larger diameter, but it does not exceed, by very much, the mathematic limit of self-support for a spiral under full load which is determined by the material from which it is made. (I.e., wood being of lesser compressive and tensile strength than steel, but steel having a much different "bending moment" than wood.) In other words, these things are key to determine the strength of a spiral structure.

In this instance, the staircase **does have a central support** and can, in deed, support itself and a considerable load of people. The central support is the inner spiral that is of very small radius which functions as an almost solid pole. Further, the structure is strengthened by the outer stringer being attached to the inner stringer by the steps about every six inches. These steps are of triangular shape which is consistent with the mathematical divisions of a circle (radians) which add even **more distribution** of loading stresses. Also, the outer stringer is *stiffened* greatly by these steps which provide paths for forces to be transmitted to the inner stringer which is much stiffer. Finally, the steps provide many rigid braces arranged in a circular fashion spirally thus forcing the outer and inner stringers to collectively function more or less equally and simultaneously. However, some unknown person during later years has added a steel bracket at the point of attachment to the choir loft joist. But the staircase existed and functioned well for many years prior to its installation.

The springiness felt when walking on the staircase is the result of the wood's reaction to the amount of loading being applied with respect to the wood's fixed "bending" characteristics. Technically, the *bending moment* mentioned here is the point at which the wood's shape remains changed when a side load is applied to its longitudinal axis, and is the definition used here.

Actually, if one will notice carefully, the springiness is a bit more on the outer ends of the steps than on the inner ends of the steps. This differential of springiness is due to the larger diameter of the outer stringers being able to spring a bit more because the *angle* of leverage with respect to the horizontal floor allows for more "give" or bend in the wood. This would, most likely, prevent the outer stringer from standing alone. This, also, therefore, is the reason, from an engineering standpoint, the steps are fastened so accurately and carefully and strongly to **both** stringers.

SUMMARY. The *Inexplicable Stairs* **can** be explained, however it remains a mystery to we humble humans just how they got there and who built them. But I hasten to add this: No matter *who* built them, God Himself had a major hand in it. The wisdom, the knowledge of physics, carpentry, and cabinetry, plus the mighty skill of human hands are all items of total mastery of the trade. I, myself, served my apprenticeship and came to graduate as a master cabinetmaker prior to entering university at age thirty. Also, I graduated from Colorado State University after earning a professional science degree in Wood Technology Engineering and Forestry. I mention this only to lend credibility to the forgoing statement, and to say that I would be very challenged to construct such a staircase using the tools and transportation of the time. However, if the occasion should ever arise to do such a thing, as in all other things I do, I shall trust that He will give me the things I would need to do the task; I am not at all surprised nor do I doubt that this is truly a *"miraculous"* staircase.

This is truly a fine example of excellent engineering and craftsmanship and should be contemplated by all thinkers of our time and times to come.

Easley

Library of Congress Registration No. TX 4-502-503

World Copyright July 08, 1997
Forrest N. Easley
HC-2, Box 845
Gainesville, MO 65655-9215

This work published by Forrest N. Easley. All rights reserved. No part of this work may be copied or reproduced by any method or means whatsoever without written permission of the author. Al rights of translation are reserved.

Printed in the USA, First edition 1997

LORETTO CHAPEL STAIRCASE WOOD

Santa Fe, New Mexico

Analysis and Technical Description

December 28, 1996

By

Forrest N. Easley
Consulting Forester/Wood Technologist

INTRODUCTION

T he following is an analytical description of the botanical properties of a small speciman of wood which was taken from the upper-inner stringer of the Loretto-Chapel staircase approximately where it joins the choir balcony front girder timber. The speciman measured three quarters of an inch squarish by one eighth-inch in thickness. I was typical of the remaining original staircase wood, and it included the "white plaster" coating which was applied many years after the staircase construction was completed.

(NOTE: When utilizing a powerful microscope, only a very small speciman of wood material is necessary because it is being magnified several hundred times to study the details of the inner structure of the wood cells and their structural relationships. Large samples are used by those who attempt identity solely by observing bark, wood grain, wood color and so on, but aren't nearly so accurate as microscopic examination.)

Since the true identity of the wood used to construct this truly beautiful and *mysterious* staircase has always been an item of conjecture and mystery, every effort to honestly examine and study the wood from every technical standpoint has been made over a period of fifteen months. Also other closely related species and genera were examined and compared as discussed in this report.

The approach to this important study was and is to approach it with a totally open mind with absolutely no personal opinions or *feelings* regards either the identity of the wood or its origin. However, it is admitted that this investigator, although very experienced, is most humbled and gratified for being allowed this opportunity to participate in such an important study of a very Holy place such as the Loretto Chapel, especially its famous staircase. Therefore, the information presented herein is as accurate as this researcher has been able to make it and the statements made herein are totally unbiased and scientific.

Presented below is the actual highly technical description of the wood speciman from the Loretto Chapel staircase. The same format is used in its presentation as used in the _Key to Coniferous Woods_ which is appended to this description. The purpose of including the _key_ is to provide technical descriptions of closely-related genera and species of woods that were _not_ locally available at the time of construction of the staircase. These species were, and are, timber species used which are currently used for lumber and were, and are, extremely good structural materials.

Upon _close examination_ of each of these descriptive paragraphs in the _key_, one finds that there are threads of similarity among all the coniferous (evergreen) tree species. Yet, also, one notices there are certain characteristics that are markedly different between one species and its sister species of the same genus. That is to say that, for example, for the genus Picea (Spruces), there is a member of the genus with the species scientific name _sitchensis_ which bears the common name Sitka Spruce. Also, in the same genus, there is another species with the scientific name _engelmannii_ which bears the common name Engelmann Spruce. Both are beautiful spruce trees and are both very excellent lumber species. However, Engelmann Spruce was usually inaccessible to logging because it grows at much higher elevations near timberline. In addition, and more importantly, there are many microscopic differences in the wood cells themselves which set the two species apart and, thus, establish two separate species as well as differing structural qualities.

With that background, the descriptive _key_ to the physical, mechanical, and non-mechanical characteristics is presented.

KEY TO THE WOOD IN THE LORETTO STAIRCASE

Based on Gross and Minute Features

The microscopic technical characteristics of the speciman wood sample from the staircase in the Loretto Chapel in Santa Fe, New Mexico were examined under a variable-power hand lens for general characteristics and under a powerful compound microscope at the magnifications varying between 50X to 450X.Both macroscopic and microscopic views of the cross sections and longitudinal samples were observed, and the intracellular characteristics were compared to other similar genera and species in an effort to positively identify and isolate this speciman. Comparative data were taken from university-level texts used at the College of Forest Sciences, Colorado State University as well as the investigator's long experience in similar studies and reporting.

First, the sample was studied and, after determining its basic characteristics, was placed in its proper position in the key list of plants, a key which has been long used by professional botanists, foresters, and colleges of forestry and forest sciences was used here. The wood was determined to be "cone-bearing" and "evergreen" with an "unjointed woody stem".

A further step to a more exacting identity required the examination of the internal structure of the cellular arrangement and function. As can be seen in the following descriptive key, only one genus in indicated **PICEA (Spruce)**

At the end of the key, is presented a summary of this study and a table of comparative data that presents the features of related species in an effort to show any relationship of the sample speciman under study to the "known" tree species named and are described in approved and professionally accepted documents and publications.

As was noted, no specific species is indicated. But a wood (an undiscovered species) is indicated that fits <u>between</u> Picea sitchensis and Picea engelmannii.

Therefore, I, the investigator, hereby assign the following names to the thus-far unnamed species within the genus Pinacae Picea (The Spruces): LORETTO SPECIMAN: Suggested SCIENTIFIC name: Picea josefii Easley

Suggested Common Name: Loretto Spruce

The Loretto specimen keys out as follows:

Wood Non-porous (no vessels). Cross sections consist of radial rows of tracheids distinctly visible; rays are present and appear distinct also to the naked eye.

Resin canals present. Longitudinal canals appear as small openings mostly in the outer portion of the late wood. Transverse canals included in some rays then appear much larger, but sparse, and under a microscope **appear as small donuts** with a dark outer margin. This is typical to the Picea genus (spruces).

Resin canals numerous, unevenly distributed in the outer portion of every growth ring, generally visible to the naked eye, as light-colored dots or small openings; conspicuous with a hand lens. Epithelial cells are thin-walled.

Tangential surface (split) WAVY (not dimpled or undimpled as in other Picea species). Outer margin of growth increment not distorted.

Wood very strong, light to moderately heavy. Bands of

late wood usually narrow and pinkish in color. Early wood light-tan to light-brown. Late wood forming a band 5 to 10 cells in width.

Heartwood light reddish to light brown. Resin canals small, inconspicuous or not visible to the naked eye. The majority of the resin canals are with a tangential diameter less than 100 um, no visible ray tracheid dentations or, at least, not prominent, not extending across the cell.

Ray parenchyma cross-field pits in early wood small, and occur fewer than 5 per cross field.

Late wood not pronounced. Transition from early wood to late wood is gradual but noticeable.

Heartwood distinct but gradual. Wood as an entity is light-brownish to pinkish tinge at the late wood and is semi-lustrous, fine textured, and the tangential (split) surface is **not dimpled, but wavy.**

Longitudinal tracheids are more or less <u>square</u> in cross section. Average dimension of 20 to 25 um on each side when viewed in a radial section of wood under a microscope.
